Fifty Works of
English* Literature
We Could Do Without

* and American

by **BRIGID BROPHY** / **MICHAEL LEVEY** / **CHARLES OSBORNE**

STEIN AND DAY/*Publishers*/New York

Fifty Works of

English* Literature

We Could Do Without

* and American

TO
Ken Thomson

First published in the United States of America
by Stein and Day/*Publishers,* 1968

Copyright © 1967 Brigid Brophy, Michael Levy, Charles Osborne

Library of Congress Catalog Card No. 68-13491

Stein and Day/*Publishers*/7 East 48 Street, New York, N. Y. 10017

Contents

Address to the Reader

BEFORE you let fly with a scream at our iconoclasm, pause and play fair: do you *really* like, admire and (most important criterion of all) enjoy the works in question, or do you merely think you ought to?

English Literature, as it is presented by pundits to enquiring persons, is choked with the implied obligation to like dull books. In making a start on weeding it, we have been moved by our sense of the injustice done alike to great authors and to the public.

It must often happen that a young person takes up or has forced on him one of the accepted 'classics'; he finds it either blatant tripe or unreadable; and he thereupon decides he is through with English Literature as a whole. In fact, if he is discriminating enough to be bored by Ben Jonson, he is likely to be the very person who would most vividly respond to Marlowe, Shakespeare and Webster; if he finds Gray insipid, he is the more likely to take fire from Donne, Crashaw, Marvell and Pope; if he's irked by the emotional and imaginative feebleness of *Ivanhoe* or *The Vicar of Wakefield*, he is probably – but without knowing it – crying out for the adult, imaginative vision of Henry James, Shaw, Jane Austen, the Thackeray of *Vanity Fair*, Gibbon and George Eliot.

Yet how *can* he know it, so long as dross and works of genius carry the same label of 'classic'? To perpetuate the received opinions about English Literature is to force our children into philistinism, even when philistinism is against their natural bent, and at the same time to cheat our great writers of even the posthumous justice which is usually, and by tradition, the best that our society is prepared to offer them.

We quite realize that about tastes there is no absolute arbitrating and that the opinions of the three of us are as liable to error as the opinions we claim to correct. But our taste is, at least, felt and scrutinized, not merely inherited from tradition and schooling. Luckily, to argue for the demotion of a work of literature does not physically destroy or deface it, as sometimes happens to buildings, statues and paintings when taste turns against them – though a heavy fall of received opinion can obscure a book almost as thoroughly and irretrievably as if it were destroyed. Neither do we exercise the tyrannical power of a magistrate – who, when he opines that a book is 'obscene' and without literary merit, orders its destruction, with the intolerant result that his fellow-citizens cannot read it to see whether they agree with his opinion. If our opinions are wrong, it is easy to discount them. We are, after all, only three, against the whole weight of received opinion.

We have written this book on the principle enunciated by Coleridge: 'Praises of the unworthy are felt by ardent minds as robberies of the deserving.'

*

We have taken the 'English' in 'English Literature' to be describing a language, not a nation. American literature is therefore included.

We have, on the other hand, excluded translations. That is why the Bible is not listed.

We accept collective, Cabinet-fashion responsibility for all the opinions expressed, but the entries themselves are not composite jobs; each is by one of us, and each of us has undertaken about a third of the total number. The entries are in (roughly) the chronological order of the birth of the authors of the works concerned. None of the authors is living.

We haven't bothered with stuffed owls. We make no entries for (i) works which are famous (or notorious) solely for being bad; (ii) works of acknowledged but entertaining tripe; and (iii)

the generally acknowledged failures of great writers, such as
Titus Andronicus and *Romola*. With possibly one exception, all
the books we deal with are revered or treated as required reading
– in the current academic syllabus, in current 'guides' meant for
the general public or in the current critical consensus.

*

We have been at pains both in this preliminary address and
throughout our text to indicate which the blooms are for whose
sake we want to clear the weeds. Indeed, if you will go so far
as actually to read our text, you will find that quite a lot of it
consists of literary appreciation. In any case, the popular distinction between 'constructive' and 'destructive' criticism is a sentimentality: the mind too weak to perceive in what respects the
bad fails is not strong enough to appreciate in what the good
succeeds. To be without discrimination is to be unable to praise.
The critic who lets you know that he always looks for something
to like in works he discusses is not telling you anything about
the works or about art; he is saying 'see what a nice person I am'.

That a book is not mentioned among the weeds does not necessarily imply we absolve it of being one. Indeed, our present choice
of fifty works from English Literature is made without prejudice
to our choosing, in the future, further examples from perhaps a
wider area of choice.

B. B.

M. L.

C. O.

Beowulf

THIS is one of those works of English [*sic*] Literature [*sic*] that fortunately most people always have done without, but it deserves its place here because of the comparatively recent tendency to stick it at the beginning of any English syllabus. Its merit lies not in its quality but in the difficulty of its text (shall we follow Klaeber's decision to accept Grundtvig's proposal as a genuine and typical example of the sort of crux it abounds in). And, of course, in its dreadful length – over 3,000 lines long. We need some respectable pseudo-Homeric epic from which to make Northern literature evolve. The poem has been called 'tough builder's work of true stone' (J. R. R. Tolkien), and this happy phrase does full justice to the work's toughness of texture, aridity and stony pugnacity. Boring and unattractive as a story, pointlessly bloodthirsty but – we are always told – fundamentally Christian, *Beowulf* is a fine example of primitive non-art. Admiring comment on its poetry is about as relevant as praise for the architecture of Stonehenge. Doubtless in the eighth century it whiled away long dreary hours in Northumbrian beerhalls, but with the disappearance of Anglo-Saxon England, and with the creation of English (proper) Literature (proper), it should now be handed over to the historians or left to be picked apart by linguistic scholars. Amid all its failures should be noted its complete inability to make one feel anything except repulsion for

Beowulf

Beowulf, its hero, and considerable sympathy for his enemies,
the monster Grendel and his mother. What starts the enmity, and
the poem, is Grendel's dislike of the noise made by the Danes
as they revel daily in their banquet hall. Thus the work opens
with the reader already biased against the mead-swilling Danes,
making a first but not final appearance in this rôle in English
literature. At Elsinore Claudius keeps wassail in the same old
noisy fashion, and Hamlet's comments on that custom aptly
apply beyond it to include the custom of honouring *Beowulf*:

> and indeed it takes
> From our achievements, though performed at height,
> The pith and marrow of our attribute.

The York Mystery Plays

NEVER look a work of art in the mouth. After all, does it matter how old it is? Yet too frequently we value the older above the newer for no better apparent reason than that it has lasted longer. This is a particular characteristic of the English temperament. How reverently we gaze at almost any Gothic cathedral: how perplexed and untempted we are by the glitter of Baroque. How stirred by Gregorian chant: how unmoved by the more sophisticated art of Handel. Yet, in the centuries between Gregorian chant and Handel, between Gothic and baroque, the arts of music and architecture have made tremendous leaps forward in technique and complexity. It can only be this absurd nostalgia for the remote past, this mindless yearning towards primitivism, towards the time when art was so simple it was not art, which is responsible for the modern interest in and production of the various cycles of mystery plays which flourished in medieval England. The cycle which has come down to us, as they say, almost in its entirety is the York Cycle of Mystery Plays. This originally consisted of fifty-seven different varieties of play, each performed by a guild of tradesmen, such as the barbers, the goldsmiths, the coopers, the butchers, the pewterers. On Corpus Christi day the plays were trundled around the city in carts, acted by the tradesmen who were no doubt as awful, but let us hope as funny, as Shakespeare's 'rude mechanicals'. Rude and mechanical the plays certainly are, and it is astonishing that modern criticism has elected to take them seriously. Again, the veneration for what is old, or older. That we should find anything to admire in the dismally primitive technique of the authors of the mystery plays, written nearly two hundred years before English theatre began to be of any real interest, is a sad reflection on the frivolity of modern taste.

The York plays were crude religious propaganda and, no doubt, ideally suited to the intellectual capacities of the credulous citizenry before whom they were performed. Religious propaganda, as such, is not to be despised. It can sometimes be great art as well. But the Bach *St Matthew Passion*, Verdi's *Requiem*, the Karlskirche in Vienna and the sculpture of Michelangelo are a far cry from the cynically concocted doggerel of a committee of drunken monks at St Mary's Chapel, York, in 1350. They *must* have been drunk : the preponderance of alliterative verse in the plays points to this. Alliteration is most frequently resorted to in intoxication.

The alliteration in the York plays pounds on so determinedly that it is sometimes impossible either to read or declaim the lines with any degree of seriousness. In his opening speech in *The Barkers' Play* God himself resorts to this kind of utterance :

Unto my dignity dear shall duly be dight
A place full of plenty at my pleasure to ply.

And the tipsy monks can do no better for the pride of Lucifer than :

I am glorious and great, and figured full fit.
The form of fairness upon me lies fast.
All wealth I am wielding, so wise is my wit,
The beams of my brightness are built with the best.

This is the kind of thing that a couple of hundred years later Shakespeare could parody so brilliantly when he wanted to. Today we are apparently expected to admire it. But it is not only the verse technique in the Mystery Plays that is a matter for ridicule. The characterization, as one might imagine, is non-existent. As a monument to the crudity of life and religious thought in medieval times, the York Mystery Plays may have some value. As works of theatrical art they are too feeble to be considered.

EDMUND SPENSER

The Faerie Queene

PROBABLY no one has actually read every line of *The Faerie Queene*, but it's an enduring monument (in misapplied Gothic style, with Elizabethan topknot) of English Literature. We need it, and make use of it, as our major contribution to the Renaissance epic. How else would the pundits be able to contrast and discuss relations with Ariosto and Ronsard did we not have a native product to make the perfect examination question? Besides, the punishing length, utter confusion and unremitting tedium of Spenser's contribution serve not merely to impress uncreative minds but to illustrate generally that Eng. Lit. is not an easy option. Its distasteful tone and ungainly bulk are the very secret of its enduring success. A monument remains a monument even when its style is uncouth and it itself rarely visited. The wilful insanity of the devisors of Eng. Lit. at Oxford has probably long been apparent, but is neatly expressed in their choice of Spenser to share a whole examination paper with Milton – the only two poets, Shakespeare apart, honoured in this way.

It must be admitted that few poems lend themselves better than *The Faerie Queene* to the examination system. It is impossible not to catch out candidates on either the language or the story – both of which are preposterous to the point of incomprehensibility. The defence of the *Faerie Queene* rests on the feeble ground that nothing quite like it had been attempted before in English. Here is a typical professorial explanation of part of Book III : 'It is an exercise in ingenuity rather than an appeal to the supra-rational imagination, decorative rather than evocative of thought, but it has rarely been better done than by Spenser.' In so far as this means anything at all, it suggests a competition by poets to be ingenious and decorative without evoking any response in the reader's intellect or imagination. In such a competition Spenser will certainly always be the victor.

The poem's confusions begin with Spenser himself. It is partly a Christian allegory, partly a political one, partly a 'poetic' poem with literary allusions and partly a would-be snobbish defence of being a Protestant English gentleman. Perhaps. for some of these reasons, it remains unfinished. It is written in a language which perfectly accords with its sentiments, and aptly defined by Ben Jonson as 'no Language'. Spenser is the very opposite of Chaucer not only in poetic quality but in his desire to make the English language as defiled and grotesquely obscure as possible. Anything resembling clarity, wit, strength of verse, is banished. It is not replaced by any proto-Miltonic massiveness and dignity. Instead, Spenser delights in archaicisms that themselves are not even genuine, coinages of a mind that will invent the obscurities it cannot find elsewhere. The story [sic] follows the same rule, combining obscurity and absurd incident with a thread of insipidity in sentiment which is most typical of the author. The chastity he extols is the virginal shrinking not of an English woman but an English public-school boy; and it is to this model that the whole poem is constructed, with focal points on the Chapel, Clean Living, and the Royal Family.

To some extent Spenser was therefore wise to wrap up his sentiments in the cheapest tinsel of allegory which he could devise. As a politician, he must have seemed best qualified to be a poet – and to be that was his real endeavour. Poetry was to him not so much a discipline as a luxury, slurred into being 'poesy' where you just scribble down in your own private language monotonous rhyming verses which run endlessly on, never sparkling into inspiration but, alas, apparently inexhaustible :

And after, all the raskall many ran,
Heaped together in rude rabblement,

To see the face of that victorious man:
Whom all admired, as from heaven sent. . . .

To those who have neglected or remained ignorant of Chaucer, Donne, Marvell, Pope and Keats, this may indeed seem poetry, and worthy stuff to be inculcated as part of the rich heritage of English literature. Spenser himself seemed to have had a flash of the true facts when he wrote to Sir Walter Raleigh, explaining 'the whole intention of the conceit', without which he thought the work might well seem 'tedious and confused'. He placed too great assurance on the explanation. His own verdict turns out to be the truest and shrewdest ever made on *The Faerie Queene*.

The Alchemist

PERHAPS it is unnecessary to set, here, the seal on Jonson's reputation. After all, T. S. Eliot begins an essay in *Elizabethan Dramatists* thus: 'The reputation of Jonson has been of the most deadly kind that can be compelled upon the memory of a great poet.' And an American critic, Harry Levin, refers to him as 'the greatest unread English author', as someone who has always received more attention from antiquarians than from critics. But both Eliot and Levin make obeisance to the idea of Jonson's 'greatness', and the time has now come for it to be spelt out carefully that Jonson was no great poet, and that a reverent bowing of the head at each mention of his name is no longer obligatory.

It is true, as Eliot says, that no critic has succeeded in making Jonson appear pleasurable or even interesting. The astonishing thing is that anyone should try. One has only to compare him with the other Elizabethans, Beaumont, Fletcher, Marlowe, Webster, not to mention Shakespeare, to realize immediately that he is not of their stature. Each of those other playwrights, even at his worst, offers the immediate excitement of vigorous language, of poetry, of superb theatrical effect. Jonson's arid intelligence provides none of these delights. His scholarship may be secure, but his thought is conventional and his verse laboured. His attempts to write tragedy resulted in grotesque failure, but the opinion is still frequently expressed that in *Bartholomew*

The Alchemist

Fair, Volpone and *The Alchemist*, Jonson produced three suc-
cessful comedies. This foul rumour has no factual foundation :
the man must have a heart of stone who could raise a laugh at,
for instance, *Volpone*, whose clumsy, heavy-handed satire is
expressed in the deadest of language.

Jonson's academic style is at the furthest remove from poetry.
Eliot, when he wishes to praise Jonson as a poet, can only point
to a passage, claim it is 'related to' Marlowe and that, if Marlowe
is a poet, then Jonson is also. This illogical nonsense can be
exposed simply by reading any of the comedies. The manner
may well occasionally owe something to Marlowe, but it has
nothing of his delicacy, his wit, or his blazing inspiration. It is
superficial bombast. Jonson's classical lack of interest in character and in motivation, and his concern with 'humours', in an
age when Shakespeare had shown what the drama was capable
of achieving, combine inexorably with the dullness of his
language to brand him as the great Elizabethan non-poet and
non-playwright. And nowhere are all these qualities displayed
with more admirable clarity than in *The Alchemist*. The plot is
uninteresting, and is hardly animated by the pedantry of the
verse in which it is exposed. The plainly didactic purpose irritates.
The play has no development, either of incident or of character.
So charmlessly pronounced is its lack of personality that it might
have been conceived by a computer. When one has remarked
that *The Alchemist* is a satire on gullibility, one has exhausted
its interest. It may be a worthy treatise; it is most assuredly a
worthless play.

WILLIAM SHAKESPEARE

Hamlet, Prince of Denmark

THERE is a fatality in public taste which, faced with an author so ineffably great that he cannot be ignored, often contrives to pick on and treat as 'central' his weakest or nearly weakest work. Such slight examples of James's art as *The Aspern Papers* and *Washington Square* are probably better known than *The Golden Bowl*; the masterworks of Bernard Shaw, *Back To Methuselah* and *Heartbreak House*, are adored only by professing Shavians, whereas everyone (thanks, probably, to the school syllabus) knows, and even scoffers grant greatness to, *Saint Joan*, an inept village-pageant in too many tableaux, most of them (oh, that 'poetic' passage between Dunois and that kingfisher) worked in pre-Raphaelite cross stitch.

Similarly with the plays of Shakespeare. It is quite true that *Hamlet* is a crucial monument in western civilization and its eponymous prince a universal figure, of whom we all, like Coleridge, have a smack ourselves. In fact Hamlet is the posturing, self-pitying, egotistical baby-cum-adolescent in us all, and the play is the prototype of western literature's most deplorable and most formless form, autobiographical fiction. The whole of *Hamlet* is seen through Hamlet's eyes.

This situation need not overbalance a play if the dramatist is frank – that is, expressionist – about it (as in *Peer Gynt*) or if the ego-character can, like Richard II, draw us by the magic of poetry into such sympathy with him that his self-pity becomes identified with our pity. *Hamlet*, however, is ostensibly an objective, naturalistic, conversational play; and it is therefore vitiated by Hamlet's vampirism.

When Hamlet presumes to actually write the other characters' lines for them, as he does by his device of running up some speeches (and atrocious speeches they are) for the Player King and Queen, or when he actually deprives them of speech at all, as he does by reducing them to pantomime in *The Mousetrap*, he is merely underlining, by dramatizing it, the injury he has already done. For he has already sucked all the independent life out of every other character in the play. It's not enough for him to hog the stage, periodically clearing it of everybody else and holding up the action so that he can give vent to his soliloquies; it's not enough to bait an old man in order to show off his own wit (e.g. the hard-breathing puns of 'it was a brute part of him to kill so capital a calf there') and to display his own interesting psychic wounds (and he seems to think it's another of *his* wounds when by a blunder he casually murders the old man): Hamlet is so jealous lest anyone else attract our attention and sympathy that he forces the girl he claims to love into the most stultified and unactable rôle Shakespeare ever wrote, reduces Claudius to pasteboard and Gertrude to suet (Gertrude who is one of Shakespeare's potentially most interesting characters) and obliges Horatio, for whom he professes friendship, to be so wet and square that his entire character can be designed only to show off Hamlet's scintillations.

Indeed Hamlet, failed poet and dramatist himself, is actually envious of Shakespeare, whose native melodiousness is in this one play cramped and lamed. The sense in which we 'can do without' *Hamlet* is less absolute than that in which we can do without the other forty-nine works listed in this volume – it is in the sense that we could do with more of the truly great plays. Do the English deserve the poet of *Antony and Cleopatra*, *A Midsummer Night's Dream* and the Sonnets, when they pick on *Hamlet* as his cardinal work and, out of the whole of *Hamlet*, 'To be or not to be' as the cardinal speech? – a speech whose opening four lines halt their way through four feminine endings and include the reiterated—er—er, the stutter in blank verse, of 'WhethER 'tis noblER in the mind to suffER'.

Goodnight, ovER-rated prince.

JOHN BUNYAN

Pilgrim's Progress

BUNYAN's delayed and prolonged adolescent religious crisis at the age of twenty not only completely ruined his own life but also urged into being one of the most heavily unreadable 'great works' with which our literature is studded. Driven almost to madness by the absurd and ferocious biblical texts he studied so assiduously, he was bullied first into conversion and then into the fanatical desire to convert others. Inexperienced, illogical, and single-minded to the point of lunacy, he was equipped for nothing but preaching. Made to 'cease from preaching and evangelizing and conform to the worship of the Church of England', he – with a blandly unflinching cruelty to posterity – wrote out his vast sermon at unendurably gigantic length. If we claim to like his allegorical farrago, we deserve to be condemned and branded as dilettantes. For, morality being a mere branch of aesthetics, no book that is morally so warped can in any real sense be aesthetically satisfying.

It is devoutly to be wished that, through the writing of *Pilgrim's Progress*, Bunyan achieved considerable cathartic release from the psychological hell into which his notions of religion had plunged him; but it is impossible to rate his naive and fevered imagination any higher than that of the gentlemen who walk through the West End of London with sandwich-boards imploring us to flee from the wrath to come. Take their boards away from them, and they too might produce *Pilgrim's Progress*.

13

Written as much to bolster his wavering faith as to confound his enemies, Bunyan's monstrous tract, despite its author's maniacal squabbles with established ecclesiastical authority, is a curious monument to frightened conformity. His sad attempt to objectify his psychopathic fears by turning them into real characters fails, because they were never sufficiently meaningful to survive projection upon the wide screen of the outside world.

That this uneducated bigot wrote an occasionally tolerable prose is of little importance. Tolerable it is, but nowhere does it strike or exhilarate. There are livelier and more amusing expositions available of the Calvinist doctrine that we are all predestined to either salvation or damnation. Bunyan's folksy grandeur of style is hardly suited to his subject. Nor, for that matter, are his characters. His hero Christian, fleeing from his wife and children, putting his fingers in his ears so as not to hear their entreaties, and rushing off shouting 'Life, life, eternal life', has his modern counterpart not in the philosophical thinkers but in the harassed suburban husband who deserts his family for the sake of a suddenly revealed mission in life, which is probably something like saving souls on Wimbledon Common. This seventeenth-century Billy Graham hasn't the intellectual energy to sustain an argument throughout the length of his narrative. His tired martial metaphors might pass in a brief oral harangue from the pulpit, but not on the printed page and at such length. His allegory is clumsy, and frequently breaks down. When it does, Bunyan appears not to notice, but picks himself up and stumbles on.

The temptation to list his shortcomings in detail must be resisted. His mechanical story plods its predetermined way, leaving even the hardiest of his readers fallen by the wayside. No book, not even one with such pious claims to greatness, has the right to be as dull as this. It could be excused only if its moral argument were of great relevance to us today. It is, of course, not.

Bunyan's language, we are sometimes told, stems from the Authorized Version of the Bible. A likelier provenance, it seems to us, is the clumsier prose of Shakespeare. The author's verse preface to *Pilgrim's Progress* certainly derives from the Bard, but unfortunately it's the kind of verse Shakespeare wrote for the Athenian clowns in their play of *Pyramus and Thisbe*. Here, as a sort of bonus, are a few lines of Bunyan the poet:

Thus I set pen to paper with delight,
And quickly had my thoughts in black and white.
For having now my method by the end,
Still, as I pulled it came, and so I penned
It down, until it came at last to be
For length and breadth the bigness which you see.

DANIEL DEFOE

Moll Flanders

DEFOE-FIELDING-SMOLLETT constitute English Literature's belt of Stockbrokers' Georgian. Red-faced as the brick houses of the period, but quite without their elegance and form, these novelists are called by admirers 'Hogarthian' and 'robust' (though, deeply considered, neither of those adjectives is quite unambiguous praise) and might be characterized by non-admirers as practitioners of the Old Brutalism.

Within that belt, Defoe represents ribbon development. *Moll Flanders* is the thinnest conceivable trickle of narrative. In its passage from Moll's birth to her settling, reformed and in a mood to live happily ever after, in the American colonies, the narrative meanders, certainly, but acquires neither breadth nor depth. It could be said to leave nothing out. More exactly, it puts nothing in. It just makes stark, unrealized, undramatized, ungraphic statements, with never an attempt to evoke personality, relationships or atmosphere. No more does it indicate Defoe's moral attitude. He may equally well be deploring, enjoying or standing indifferent to the social brutality he – in so offhand and condensed a way – records. His moral awareness and his story-telling are alike stunted, and neither is to be excused by his being 'early' among English novelists. (*Moll Flanders* dates from 1722, though it is, like Defoe's *Journal of the Plague Year*, an historical novel; Moll's narrative purports to have been written in 1683.)

In Defoe's own period, Pope was already sensitive to human

17

brutality even towards animals; and two and a half centuries earlier Malory had spun graphic, quirky prose narrative from an English language far less sophisticated than Defoe could command. True, Defoe writes a clean, unpretending prose, but it's a prose quite inept to novels, since it swallows all the vividness of what it recounts into itself, like an exercise converting direct into indirect speech. 'They did get into the house by main force, and broke up the locked place where the watches were. . . . But the family, being alarmed, cried out "Thieves", and the man was pursued and taken; the young woman had got off too, but unhappily was stopped at a distance.' That's a fine way for a clerk of the court, but no way for a novelist, to describe something as exciting as burglary.

Tom Jones

MUCH of English literary life and probably some of English literature have been marred by the public school tradition whereby a boy became 'literary' not because he was good at and interested in literature but because he was bad at, though not uninterested in, games. *Stalky & Co.* both describes and exemplifies the process: an inky boy who wears glasses becomes a writer *faute de mieux* and writes about the admiration he feels for Stalky because Stalky isn't short-sighted and is too illiterate to run much risk of getting ink on his hands. Perhaps because they expect other people to assume that they are literary through some disability elsewhere, perhaps because they even suspect this to be true themselves, many English men of letters seem to feel a particular vulnerability to the accusation that they are weedy, anaemic and somehow less in touch with real life than more robust persons who put their life-energy into putting footballs into touch. Against that accusation, *Tom Jones* has served English men of letters for two centuries as a talisman. 'We? Anaemic? But we love *Tom Jones.*' *Tom Jones* has become the accepted epitome of red-bloodedness. Literary persons entertain about it the same superstition that Fielding himself and his friend Hogarth entertained about beef: that to consume it with conspicuous gutsiness has the magic property of making you both very robust and very English – to the extent that you will be *more* English than non-beefeaters born and bred in the same country.

Tom Jones truly is a vigorous book. The trouble is where the vigour resides. It's not in Tom himself, a tom cat of remarkable passivity, who has to be seduced or flattered into his series of love affairs and finishes as tame as a *jeune premier* in a Doris Day musical, married to the girl next door with full parental blessing. Fielding is justified in leaving Tom's face a blank, of which we're told only that it's handsome, full of sweetness and 'the picture of health'; but he might have made a slightly more distinctive job of Tom's personality. Yet, you might suppose, Tom's personality is intended for a bare thread stringing together picaresque adventures – were it not that the adventures range so unadventurously in both place and theme. They are not much more than an alternation of beddings and thumpings, without much of the sensuous feel of either; the suspicion that Tom may have committed incest goes unexploited for horror, comedy, irony or melodrama even before it turns out to be a misunderstanding of the facts anyway. Then the vigour must lie in the supporting cast, the genre characters? But they turn out to *be* characters only on the sandwich-flag system. Each gets either a single speech characteristic (dialect for the squire, tags of bad Latin and Greek for Partridge) or an allegorical name: Thwackum, Sophia, Allworthy – whose allworthiness does not prevent him from believing ill of Tom on insufficient evidence or from the snobbery of thinking better of him when he turns out to have been born from the same social class as Allworthy himself.

The secret is that the vigour is all in the narrative – or, rather, in the monologue. 'Narrative' implies getting on with telling the story, and that is what Fielding's monologue confesses itself most reluctant to do. 'Reader, I think proper, before we proceed any farther together, to acquaint thee, that I intend to digress, through this whole history, as often as I see occasion.' The promise is kept. Even when you reach Book Seventeen, you come on a chapter labelled 'Containing a Portion of Introductory Writing'. *Tom Jones* is virtually all introductory writing.

When he absolutely has to advance the story, Fielding does so in a perfunctory, under-realized summary. If it is true, as his admirers claim, that he learned from his experience of writing for the stage, what he learned was the writing of stage directions

too crammed and cramped to be more than memos to the pro-
ducer. 'During this dialogue Mr Nightingale took his leave, and
presently after Mrs Miller left the room, when Allworthy likewise dispatched Blifil.' Elsewhere Fielding seems to have learnt,
from his experience as a magistrate, to record events in Defoe's
clerk-of-the-court manner. In some passages his hero's strange
passivity seems to have infected the very mood of his verbs. 'A
consultation was now entered into, how to proceed in order to
discover the mother. A scrutiny was first made into the characters
of the female servants of the house . . . and perhaps it would be
difficult to find such another set of scarecrows. The next step was
to examine among the inhabitants of the parish; and this was
referred to Mrs Wilkins . . . Matters being thus settled, Mr Allworthy withdrew to his study.'

But when it's not busy keeping the minutes of his book in this
way, Fielding's monologue does indeed display the vigour it's
credited with. The monologue is conducted by an 'I' ('it will,
I question not, appear strange to many readers'), who occasionally becomes 'we' ('Before we relate what now passed . . .'). But
the 'I' is no more characterized than the Reader he so pertina-
ciously apostrophizes or the hero he is ostensibly writing about.
Fielding's 'I' no more resembles the moonlit personality of Sterne's
'I' than his digressions are inspired by Sterne's surrealism. How,
then, does the 'I' manage to fill so many pages? For if *Tom
Jones* is a little less dull in sentence-to-sentence reading than *Moll
Flanders*, it goes on, on the other hand, some ten times as long.
These innumerable pages the narrator in fact fills simply with
verbal facetiousness. He chases his own tail in the simple sense
that too many words are chasing too little tale. Fielding expects
the contortions that result to be funny. 'This matter, then, which
put an end to the debate mentioned in the last chapter, was no
other than a quarrel between Master Blifil and Tom Jones, the
consequence of which had been a bloody nose to the former . . .
A difference arising at play between the two lads, Master Blifil
called Tom a *beggarly bastard*. Upon which the latter, who was
somewhat passionate in his disposition, immediately caused that
phaenomenon in the face of the former, which we have above
remembered.'

When you emerge from reading *Tom Jones*, you *haven't* met
'a gallery of sharply observed characters', you *haven't* met an

idiosyncratic narrator, you *haven't* been conducted through an exciting story, you *haven't* savoured the sights and smells of eighteenth-century England, you *haven't* made a robust square meal. Even the smell and taste of that famous beef aren't allowed to reach your senses direct. Fielding interposes his own facetiousness: 'Indeed it may be doubted, whether Ulysses, who by the way seems to have had the best stomach of all the heroes in that eating poem of the Odyssey, ever made a better meal. Three pounds at least of that flesh which formerly had contributed to the composition of an ox, was now honoured with becoming part of the individual Mr Jones.' All you've in fact done is spend twenty-four hours in the company of an indefatigable raconteur who believes he has a gift for telling you in a funny way what it *would have* been like *had* you met those people, undergone those adventures, and experienced those tastes and smells. Vigorous this raconteur certainly is: he hasn't let up during the whole twenty-four hours in his roaring at you, slapping your back and nudging your ribs. If he's vigorous, you're exhausted. Literary persons who are secretly ashamed of being literary may now go to bed as aching and bruised as they would have been had they spent the time playing rugby.

THOMAS GRAY

Elegy Written in a Country Churchyard

THIS is Gray's Elegy, for all the world as if thousands of rival poets had *their* elegies. And even if they had, there is now no hope for them; the elegy belongs to Gray as inevitably as the Wells to Sadler. It is in the same way something of a non-existent landmark, despite its tremendous fame. Many people must have been tempted to push further into Gray's world and see if he ever produced other poems which failed only by bad luck to get into *The Golden Treasury* (q.v.). The first shock is that a great deal of his other verse *is* in that anthology – including the remarkable Pindaric Ode on the progress of Poesy (always an unfortunate word but nothing like so disastrous as Gray's Ode on it). Its penultimate line neatly crystallizes the essential priggish-ness of the author – 'Beyond the limits of a vulgar fate' – and conveys his perpetual effect of being one who not only writes in mittens but is capable of knitting them for a favourite nephew. That theme is very much of a type to encourage the genteel muse of Gray, offering ample opportunity to clothe the obvious in the well-bred banal. He certainly managed to write (or, as he would say, pen) the funniest defence of the English public school; the Ode on a distant prospect of Eton College ends 'where ignorance is bliss/ 'Tis folly to be wise'.

The use of elaborate poetic diction can be effortlessly justified by fine results; Milton and Pope are there to prove the point. Gray brought to his verse not merely the by then shop-soiled vocabulary of greater men' but a poverty of thought that is entirely his own. The dignified noise of the 'Elegy' may make it seem to be about something; but the individual lines, when examined, give the lie to such an assumption. It is not so much sheer ludicrousness which dissolves the poet's statement that no more shall the rude forefathers of the hamlet be roused from their lowly bed as the impossibility of their ever having been *roused* by 'The breezy call of incense-breathing morn'. It is this brainlessness which prompts Gray to ask questions like 'Can Honour's voice provoke the silent dust'. Only Gray, incidentally, would have thought dust needed to be described as silent.

A thread of coherence and the requirements of length are pre-served – just – by asking this sort of question and by whole quatrains which grandiloquently express the lot that was *not* the rude forefathers'. Gradually obscurity settles about the syntax as the poem takes wing into sublimity:

> E'en from the tomb the voice of Nature cries,
> E'en in our ashes live their wonted fires.

It is not possible to discover, as Dr Johnson might have re-marked, who is referred to by 'their' – unless the forefathers, and it would still remain baffling how their fires (wonted or not) live in our ashes. The youth unknown to fame and fortune has equally baffling behaviour, induced probably by the extraordin-ary countryside in which he lies and drops and roves: he was usually to be seen at dawn going to an upland lawn; by noon he was stretched under a *nodding* beech tree beside a brook. The youth's epitaph betrays similar confusion. There seems no parti-cular point to 'Fair Science frown'd not on his humble birth'. Is this a way of saying she favoured him, or that along with hundreds of others, fortunately unlisted, personifications, she was not involved in his career? His after-life is the most puzzling of all. His merits and frailties are reposing 'in trembling hope' in a 'dread abode' which is finally revealed as the bosom of God. What more can they be hoping for, and why are they trembling?

Perhaps they have an uneasy sense that they should no more be there than should Gray's Elegy be found among any list of the best poems in English Literature.

She Stoops to Conquer

GOLDSMITH had a great reputation for amusing children. If children are to be equated with uncritical innocence and merry stupidity, it is perhaps true to say that *She Stoops to Conquer* will amuse children. Even the most naive of adults can hardly be expected to find Goldsmith's play even tolerable. Recently it has been described by a Professor of English Literature at Leeds as 'timeless', which suggests merely how slowly things must move in Leeds; Goldsmith himself (always inclined to blurt out the truth) was nearer the mark when he described his play as a 'slight performance'. Following Leeds professorial standards we would have to call Tony Lumpken 'a great comic creation'. Better to accept contemporary reaction to Goldsmith's efforts at character drawing and concur with Horace Walpole who shrewdly noted how none of the characters says a sentence that is natural or 'marks any character at all'. As farce the play must now seem ponderous in its intrigue and contrived in its complexity of plot (contrived but pathetically simple). As comedy it is yet more clumsy and graceless. At the heart of Goldsmith himself there is an uncertainty about how to harness creative power to any distinct purpose. He can never sharpen his style, or his observation, to a sufficiently incisive edge. No sooner does the thought of being keen occur to him than he thinks he ought also to be kind. For ever dithering about whether to pick up a scalpel or a powderpuff, he never found the right instrument to carve out a piece of pure art. It is this inner vacillation that leads to the uncertain tone of the writings. The real feebleness of *She Stoops to Conquer* comes from its uncommittedness. There is no vigour in its clumsiness, no elegance in its style, no driving force in its plot which would carry us over its insipid characterization. The child, as it were, of Voltaire *and* Rousseau, its author cannot recover from a literary education as confused and ill-disciplined as was his own in real life. Goldsmith is certainly a delightful example of a charmingly good-humoured man. Equally certainly *She Stoops to Conquer* is a good-humoured play. But what is attractive in life is by no means sufficient *raison d'être* for literature. A particularly British sentimentality is to presume that it is, constantly mistaking the work for the man. We may want to keep Goldsmith among our English men-of-letters; let us then treat him generously and dispense with what he actually wrote.

R. B. SHERIDAN

The School for Scandal

CHARMING witty people like Sheridan live best as legends. By their work we shall not know them. Fortunate Charles James Fox, preserved somehow as a personality – perhaps the most sheerly attractive politician there has ever been, though that achievement is at best poor – without any aid from his own writings. The best of Sheridan is in Byron's response to him; and Byron knew only the prematurely old, burnt-out shell which yet occasionally still sparkled.

Knowing what we do of Sheridan's reputation it would have seemed particularly cruel had none of his plays survived. It would be easy to conceive their witty continuation of Congreve and their anticipations of Wilde – easy, if we did not have the evidence of *The School for Scandal* and *The Rivals* to show nothing of the sort. Of course, worse plays have been written by witty men (*Salome* is perhaps one of them), but few can have achieved the decorous, insipid texture of these two dreadfully famous comedies. To the brothers Surface should be added R. B. Surface – an author who in *The Rivals* is clumsy and unconvincing and in *The School for Scandal* is neat and still unconvincing. His characters are bundles of Green Room affectations, stagey types hurriedly stitched together from the most obvious materials – as exaggerated in sentimentality as in satire. But that would not matter if the results were animated by creative energy. Sheridan meant perhaps to throw off a few dramatic *jeux d'esprit,* but he restricted his range so as to avoid giving offence, tamed his *jeux* until they were not even ingenious, and was left with limp artifacts utterly lacking in any *esprit*. His well-known wish to please by emasculating was expressed most patently in the genteel re-working of Vanbrugh's *The Relapse* ('Some plays may justly call for alteration') into *A Trip to Scarborough*. *The School for Scandal* is an artificial comedy in the sense that it is constructed entirely from things that do not exist – including any sense of purpose in the author. Even as a piece of stage mechanism it is painfully clumsy, with lengthy speeches of prosy unverisimilitude inserted to keep the plot going. The *coup de théâtre* when the overturned screen in Joseph Surface's house reveals Lady Teazle is followed by almost absurd anti-climax. Lady Teazle has to exit after a speech of moral indignation so feeble that it better represents the reaction of someone jostled on a bus rather than deceived and virtually seduced by a hypocrite. The scene ends yet more feebly a few lines later when Sir Peter Teazle and Surface leave the stage while still talking.

Weak in comic invention, himself hypocritical and prudish with regard to sex – at least in literature – Sheridan cannot make any convincing gesture either in the direction of real morality or of true affection. His love passages are conventional and without heart; his comedy is broad caricature, as in Lady Sneerwell's circle where the duels of wit are conducted not with rapiers but with clubs. Ultimately there is nothing so offensive in art as the desire not to offend : it is the negation which has eaten away at Sheridan's always tiny talent and left a few piles of sand which were once – briefly – popular plays. The time has come to ring the curtain down on them. We are no longer afraid to confront the genuine wit and bawdy of Congreve and Vanbrugh. Sheridan is a milk-and-water version of the true cognac of genius; and nobody nowadays is weak enough to need his dilution.

WILLIAM WORDSWORTH

'I Wandered Lonely as a Cloud' (The Daffodils)

'THOUGH the daffodil was named in English by Shakespeare it was annexed by Wordsworth, who put his romantic trademark on it – the daffodils that *I* saw – and it is this trademark and not the name that is popularly remembered' (John Bayley).

Yes indeed. Daffodils are peddled under Wordsworth's trademark every English spring: 'Only five bob a crowd, a host, of golden daffs, love.' The implication is that to gaze and gaze at them *is* good for the health or the soul – perhaps even for the income. After all, Wordsworth claimed that gazing had brought him 'wealth'. Perhaps that's why he called those quintessentially yellow flowers 'golden'. It's harder to guess what (can it have been *just* the need of a rhyme to 'crowd'?) made him consider 'lonely as a cloud' a simile telling enough for an opening line. Lonely clouds are rare in all parts of the British Isles. In the Lake District they must be as rare as gold daffodils.

It has long been known that Wordsworth consists of both a great and an execrable poet. The point was made before the nineteenth century was out by James Kenneth Stephen, who wittily turned Wordsworth's 'Two voices' sonnet against its author and distinguished the two voices of Wordsworth himself: 'one is of the deep . . . And one is of an old half-witted sheep.' In 1879 Matthew Arnold issued the more measured warning 'we

are not to suppose that everything is precious which Wordsworth
. . . may give us'.

Recognizing the need to sift Wordsworth's oeuvre, Arnold
himself edited a volume designed 'to disengage the poems which
show his power, and to present them to the English-speaking
public'. Yet Arnold included in his selection from Wordsworth
the lines

Few months of life has he in store
As he to you will tell,
For still, the more he works, the more
Do his weak ankles swell.

Small wonder, when one of its finest critics was so unhelpful,
that the English-speaking public, though alerted to the fact that
Wordsworth *has* two voices, remains fatally muddled about which
is which.

The old half-witted sheep is, in reality, easily recognized, for
it is an old half-witted sheep done up as lamb. The worst Wordsworth is the mock-innocent Wordsworth, the one that gambols
about inviting the question 'Little William, who made thee?'
This one bleats in baa-nal rhymes *(trees-breeze)* and lisps in
nursery numbers. (The fictitious Mrs Wilson of *Mrs Wilson's
Diary* never outdid 'And then my heart with pleasure fills/And
dances with the Daffodils' for sheer lispingness.) This Wordsworth
epitomizes the fallacy of treating 'child-like' as a word of praise
for adults. He comes as near purity of heart as one of those
children's shoe departments in big stores where the walls are
papered with 'nursery rhyme characters' (look, dear, there's
Simple Simon Lee, the Old Huntsman) – with, of course, those
daffodils fluttering and dancing round the frieze. Baa-lamb
Wordsworth has the same faculty for getting the tone just wrong.
The distinction of *The Daffodils* is to have in a single stanza
expressed happiness in the three most dubious words the English
language provides for it : *glee, gay* and *jocund* – each one in its
own separate right like a prancing transfer of a woolly lamb im-
printed on the powder-pink frame of a cot.

What this pure-hearted, innocent Wordsworth is implying and,
at his extreme depths, explicitly preaching is something that
Matthew Arnold, of all people, should have detected and detes-
ted : philistinism. The bleats are out to suggest that illiteracy is

actually better than literacy – happy the childish innocent who *can* consult only the dreadful pictures, not the text. In the lines 'To my Sister, written at a small distance from my house, and sent by my little boy', the message reads in part

Edward will come with you; – and, pray,
Put on with speed your woodland dress;
And bring no book : for this one day
We'll give to idleness.

Was it, though, only one day? The poet tells us he is 'oft' in 'vacant or in pensive mood'; presumably the vacant mood accounts for quite a lot of the 'oft'. In Arnold's selection it is necessary to turn only a page to pass from the anti-book message the poet sent his sister to his complacent reply to the 'expostulation' that goes 'Why, William . . . Where are your books?' A further page, and William himself is expostulating 'Up! up! my friend, and quit your books;/Or surely you'll grow double' – precursor of all those mothers and nannies urging 'Do stop *reading*, dear – it's so *unhealthy*. Go out and gaze at daffodils.'

And indeed it is in this poem that Wordsworth explicitly enunciates his gospel of philistinism, the great anti-thought trademark he set on English life for ever after. He damns 'intellect' as 'meddling', dismisses the leaves of books as 'barren' (a phrase which, significantly, provided a title for Aldous Huxley), exclaims (could a town councillor voting against a grant for the symphony orchestra have done better?) 'Enough of Science and of Art', and promulgates the blatant lie

One impulse from a vernal wood
May teach you more of man,
Of moral evil and of good,
Than all the sages can.

The tragedy of this is that it's untrue not only to human nature but to Wordsworth's poetic nature. At his most simplicistic, in his most earnest quest for words of one syllable or, if they *must* have two, words at least of proven humdrumness (had he lived after E-nid Bly-ton, he would sure-ly have hy-phen-a-ted them), he cannot help betraying what his true talent was. Consider

No motion has she now, no force;
She neither hears nor sees;

'I Wandered Lonely as a Cloud' (The Daffodils)

> Rolled round in earth's diurnal course,
> With rocks, and stones, and trees.

If you *want* mock-simplicity, smock-simplicity, if you want 'sees'
and 'trees' rhymed and to have it spelled out to you, as distinct
and cumulative items, that the dead *neither* hear *nor* see, then
of course the whole stanza is wrecked on that orotund and Latin
'diurnal', which occupies the most pointed position in the poem
and bathetically proves to contain so little meaning (and that
little so humdrum; the diurnal round, the common task . . .). But
if you want true Wordsworth, that 'diurnal' is the only word of
his authentic uttering in the poem. For the talent Wordsworth
mortified and martyred to doctrinaire simplicity is that of one of
English literature's supreme rhetoricians. The reason Wordsworth
writes of daffodils and clouds as though he had never really set
eyes on either of them is that he is an essentially baroque artist,
to whom flowers are invisible unless transmuted into precious
metal and to whom clouds are merely what sweep apparitions
down on the astounded beholder. In his sonnets, where the metre
will not let him creak his nursery rocking-horse to and fro but
virtually obliges him to loose his native oceanic thunder, he
sounds regally clear and true as a master of Latin-derived diction and nouns used as the purely abstract personages of a vast
allegory. 'Altar, sword and pen', he finely and rhetorically roars.
Or he summons, in firm, saddened designs, a classicism that can
have come only from the books he, in his sheep-persona, despised.
True recipient of baroque visions, he really did

> Have sight of Proteus rising from the sea;
> Or hear old Triton blow his wreathed horn.

It was no peasant, no baa-lamb, who composed the loveliest
urban sonnet in English –

> This City now doth like a garment wear
> The beauty of the morning;

it was no leech-gatherer who celebrated the *pompe funèbre* of
the Venetian republic in a first line of Shakespearean splendour –

> Once did She hold the gorgeous east in fee

– and evoked 'the whole majesty of Rome' in a last line of a
baroque mass worthy of the baroque city –

'I Wandered Lonely as a Cloud' (The Daffodils)

Crowned with St Peter's everlasting dome.

When sonneteering Wordsworth re-creates the landing of Mary Queen of Scots at the mouth of the Derwent –

Dear to the Loves, and to the Graces vowed,
The Queen drew back the wimple that she wore

– he unveils nothing less than a canvas by Rubens, baroque master of baroque masters; this is the landing of a *tragic* Marie de Médicis.

Yet so receptive was the English ear to sheep-Wordsworth's perverse 'Enough of Art' that it is not any of these works of supreme art, these master-sonnets of English literature, that are sold as picture postcards, with the text in lieu of the view, in the Lake District! it is those eternally, infernally sprightly Daffodils.

The Bride of Lammermoor

WHAT can be made of a writer who at the most poignant and harrowing climax of his novel describes events only with the desperate phrase that they 'surpass description'? It is immediately obvious that we are dealing not with an artist but with Sir Walter Scott.

The non-artistry of Scott is not a matter *merely* of poverty of imagination, appalling style, insipid characterization and stunted emotional state. He is no artist by the standards not just of great novelists like Jane Austen or Henry James, but by the standards of any great writer – from Homer onwards. It is impossible to discover whether he was too lazy to try to be an artist – or whether he tried but could not succeed. His novels suggest the former; his poetry the latter. It is a double failure, largely concealed from the world by Scott's upright, honourable nature, his great fame in his lifetime, and has baronetcy. That this last was conferred for services to literature is to some people a compelling argument for believing he must have served literature; what he served it was in fact a bad turn. Only in the Kingdom of Philistia is Sir Walter Scott president of the Royal Academy of literature, but there he reigns, secure in the middle classes' affection for the non-literate writer, the one who is a great story teller with no affectations or artistic nonsense about him.

Because it is believed that Scott was a good narrative writer, he is still foisted on to children and mentioned at Christmas or in cold weather by some semi-literate journalist: still showing off his bluff, doggy face, that ghastly Abbotsford and his famous integrity. Everyone half recalls reading him as children; it's a good excuse for now not looking at his books but for retaining them in a vague limbo of nursery associations, only painfully – if at all – to be relinquished. Even E. M. Forster, who has said a few aptly harsh things about Scott, is found murmuring the old cliché: 'He had the primitive power of keeping the reader in suspense . . .'

The Bride of Lammermoor has a plot in itself rich in suspense, horrific drama and genuine pathos. According to Scott it is basically a true story, so he need be given no credit for invention. What he has done is run the story under the cold tap of his immature mind, wring it free of anything resembling suspense or passion, and then iron it out with the full starch of his genteel, highfalutin and ever-creaking style. When Ravenswood broods beside the body of a dead woman who he thinks may have appeared to him as a vision, his reflections in part run thus: 'can strong and earnest wishes, formed during the last agony of nature, survive its catastrophe, surmount the awful bounds of the spiritual world, and place before us its inhabitants in the hues and colourings of life?' The man who can think like this may be a great loss to Parliament but has clearly nothing to do with literature. Scott's vocabulary betrays the un-thinking speech-writer who deliberately clogs the meaningless with clumps of useless adjectives and solemn-seeming commas. The style remains exactly the same in tone and pseudo-literacy when the author stoops to be funny or whimsical. Much of this is mercifully obscured by the useful device of unreadable dialect. But here is Scott assuming a would-be humorous character, actually no different from the way he writes when describing [*sic*] love and death: 'For when Dick, in his more advanced state of proficiency, became dubious of the propriety of so daring a deviation from the established rules of art, and was desirous to execute a picture of the publican himself in exchange for this juvenile production, the courteous offer was refused by his judicious employer, who had observed, it seems, that when his ale failed to do its duty in conciliating his guests, one glance at his sign was sure to put them in good humour.'

This is the style of the barely educated – preferring long Latin-style words to short ones. The prosaic inability of Scott to tell his story in terms more vivid than those of a police report effectively removes any feeling of suspense or interest. Bathos not pathos is the sole sentiment he can command. Fustian dialogue is followed by scarcely believable sentences of glossing (whether to eke out the book's length or to illustrate the author's own naivety, who shall say?). At the end of *The Bride* . . . (Scott having utterly failed in haste and repugnance to convey anything of the horrific dénouement) Bucklair proudly announces his refusal ever to reveal what happened on his wedding night. For the really stupid reader or for himself, Scott adds: 'A declaration so decisive admitted no commentary.'

Scott emasculated his work, presumably deliberately, to the point where it lacks not just sexual, but any, vitality. All the emotions which go to power characters in a work of art – the passions which are no less apparent in *Emma* than in the *Iliad* – have been dehydrated and reduced to formulae. His world view is preadolescent but post-infantile. He describes what he has never consciously experienced (and hence that significant frequent need of phrases like 'surpass description') and is incapable of imagining. He can do no justice to Lucy Ashton's love for Ravenswood, still less to the Juliet-style dilemma in which that love places her. Instead, he surrounds the crux of the plot with irrelevant and in effect delaying incidents – delaying the author from having to deal with anything central or profound. Into the characters' mouths he puts dialogue that is essentially sham, more rhetorical than any situation would stimulate and more clumsy than could ever be spoken, even on the stage. It is all mouthing of emotions and descriptions of the indescribable. The result is a property cupboard of old costumes which the author *au fond* thinks are ridiculous but dons in condescending effort to entertain. He is a mountebank without a mountebank's courage, an actor who incongruously smiles at a tragic scene through his grease paint. He takes none of it seriously; as he is fond of insisting – it is all a story or history. He wants it to have happened long ago because that robs it of intensity, reality and passion: the enemies he most fears. He will waste pages on the commonplace chatter of subordinate characters and then sketch with ludicrous brevity a dramatic scene which should be given fully developed treatment.

The Bride of Lammermoor

Some people always take artists at other people's values, content to go along with the world's verdict. For them Italian opera composers are *a priori* silly, and Donizetti – over-prolific and tuneful – one of the silliest. Sir Walter Scott (also over-prolific, by the way and tuneless) is a gentleman-writer who made a lot of money and should be respected. Listen to *Lucia di Lammermoor* and then read the novel again. The Italian created a valid work of art, beside which Scott's book is revealed as the small heap of sawdust it always was.

The Essays of Elia

THERE is something in the author's very name that has a bleating irritation about it, a sort of coy pulling of wool over the eyes, a consciously innocent, over-innocent, association – all of which is quite unfair, of course, to Charles Lamb. Or is it? Lamb was by most accounts such an amusing, good-hearted – and brave – man that one would like to let the question rest, were it not for the literary work. It is not enough for Lamb to be the amusing, etc., man but he is also the creator of 'one of the masterpieces of English prose'. This considerable claim was not substantiated, it was just airily put forward without reservations by Robert Lynd. Lynd was clearly the right person to make such a claim in an introduction to the two-volume 1929 edition of the Essays. Lamb's fleece-lined mantle had by then fallen on Lynd, himself probably now forgotten but once sufficiently respected to be included in a school textbook of selected English Essays.

The essay form is one of the weakest plants in literature's garden. It promises very little, is powered by a barely creative urge, and pushes up only a few pale sprouts, leaves that are seldom accompanied by anything as positive as a flower. In some ways it is – to change the metaphor – a sort of intellectual tatting for those not strong enough to embark on a full-scale piece of work. There is Montaigne, of course, and there is Bacon. Neither perhaps, however historically or personally interesting, is quite sufficient to wipe away the stigma left by Johnson's definition of what he too wrote, the essay: an irregular, ill-digested piece. The essay's dependence on the essayist's personality is rather frightening: it never quite cuts free – as does a work of art – and gradually seems to demand more and more sustenance from the personality. It hovers on an intimacy which is false; it encourages the essayist to construct a public *persona*, usually self-deprecatory, whimsical, a lover of little things, a bit of an oddity but well aware of the literary value of being an oddity. Ultimately it becomes a genteel strip-tease which, while insisting on its artistic qualities, is aware of being sustained by vulgar human curiosity.

This makes for some uneasy moments. It is not possible to be totally guileless, candid and fully intimate in something intended as a work of art. To display those qualities you must be content with writing letters – and everyone knows the dangers of trying to write them with one eye on a public beyond the addressee. While Lamb's *Essays* are flawed by bifocal vision (among other flaws) Sydney Smith's *Letters*, for example, retain an easy unaffected homogeneity which, combined with their effortless vivacity, makes them at least approach the status of work of art. Smith instinctively creates *jeux d'esprit* which are too good not to be shared. This wit collects an audience; Lamb seems to think first of his audience and then to perform suitably in front of it, dressed up as 'Lamb', an automaton which becomes a stereotype – trailing before us his family, his friends, his foibles ('a foolish talent of mine'), until it is obvious that he is not at all guileless. Underneath is a knowing old sheep: one who is shrewd enough always to touch the audience's chord of sentimentality, shamelessly doing so in expressing an irrational love – a weakness, reader, but who without it? – for all that is past. Impossible to count the number of times emotive use is made of the word *old*: applied to china, Margate Hoy, benchers of the Inner Temple, libraries, plays, and of course friends.

This sentimental conservatism extends to the harsher facts of the world. There is no vein of Swiftian irony in Lamb's 'A Complaint of the Decay of Beggars in the Metropolis'; he is seriously sentimental about the picturesqueness of going in rags. Although even his admirers shy away from the pathetic yet mawkish 'Dream Children', they should really be more deeply disturbed by the essay on young chimney-sweepers. There was no Shaftesbury in the genteel, whimsical, ever-popular Lamb who enjoyed the sight of 'these young Africans of our own growth', and thought himself charitable in urging his readers to give them a penny. By a typical sloppiness he could not even get Shakespeare right when quoting him apropos chimney-sweeps, but had to soften the verse to read 'Golden lads and lasses must . . .' Lamb is one of those people (still richly present among us) who will defend a wrong by appealing to hallowed custom, praising the colourfulness of inequality and ever-ready to condemn as 'drab' anything that banishes poverty or child-labour.

It may be thought that Lamb was too unworldly to bother about such things; quite the opposite is the case. He was profoundly worldly and, outside his own interests, basically indifferent, even cruel. The obverse of the sentimental claptrap is a nasty joy manifested in the 'Bachelor's Complaint'. The prose has lost its facetious frills and usual coy periphrases, a welcome loss which only emphasizes the sour comment on children : 'how often they turn out ill, and defeat the fond hopes of their parents'. There is more in the same mood as we seem about to stumble the author's real nature. It is an abrupt revelation, and there are others of varying kinds. The Lamb who warmly praised Titian's *Bacchus and Ariadne* in a published Essay, wrote privately to Wordsworth that he was by no means an absolute admirer of the picture – it had merely served as illustrative of a point he wished to make.

Perhaps ultimately one prefers the private person, whatever his faults, to the increasingly rouged, positively by the end simpering, public performer whose chief stylistic contribution to English prose was to think up arch and not always intentionally funny wrapping paper to put round naked words and facts. What began as strip-tease ended up as a sort of gift shop, equipped with china ornaments of pouting children, some old brass candlesticks, and a fancy line in poker-work mottoes. The occupant of that is exactly the person to speak with inimitable roguishness, about 'that little airy musician – the lark' – and ponder where he 'doffs his night gear'.

The Confessions of an English Opium Eater

IF he were alive today, De Quincy would doubtless be engaged in writing a Patrick Campbell-like column, raking about in the detritus of his theatrically concocted personality. His hollow, glib and pompously written *Opium Eater* may well have been responsible for bringing into existence such later nineteenth-century confessions as those of Hogg, Coleridge and George Moore: what is certain is that the fizzled-out end of that line is the columnist who deliberately sets up a pitiful self to be self-pitiful about.

De Quincy is at great pains to stress that he first began to swallow opium purely in an attempt to relieve 'extremity of pain from rheumatic toothache'. Obviously, he feels guilt. Yet 'Guilt . . . I do not acknowledge' he asserts in his preface to the first edition. In fact the honesty and the self-knowledge for which he is so often praised are notoriously non-existent. This, of course, would hardly matter if what he had written were lively, entertaining and imaginative. In any case, one might reasonably have expected an account of opium addiction to possess a certain degree of excitement; but, alas, the heaviness of De Quincy's prose is equalled by that of his imagination. He is concerned to stress his uniqueness as a suffering spirit (whether suffering from toothache or from the effects of opium), and as life's victim. And, too indulgent in that direction to torture himself, he tortures the 'courteous reader' whom he apostrophizes with such condescending pomposity.

De Quincy's commentators delight in drawing our attention to his portrait of Anne, the orphaned prostitute he encountered in Oxford Street. Our attention drawn, we can only note, however, that he completely fails to bring the shadowy waif to any semblance of life, and that his attitude to her is that of a conventionally moral prig.

There remain those dreams, ostensibly opium-induced, certainly tedium-inducing. One fears they would not have been any less uninteresting had De Quincy never touched opium. A sudden, and doubtless unworthy, thought: could it be possible that he never did take opium, that it's all swiped from Coleridge, and that the *Confessions* are the pathetically unsuccessful attempt of a somewhat dull literary leech to make himself appear rather more dashing?

The Dream of Gerontius

PERHAPS it is a conspiracy between Catholic piety and misapplied tolerance on the part of non-Catholics which causes Cardinal Newman to be still cited seriously as a writer. As a saint Newman may yet have a future. As a literary artist, he should be left to Limbo.

He is, of course, a fascinating part of social history: in a social climate resembling the inside of a rather small conservatory rather overfull of intense curates breathing rather too heavily, he performed what must be the longest-drawn spiritual strip-tease in the annals of publicity. His autobiography is a valuable psychological curio, an object-lesson in how it is possible to be agonizingly honest and yet, if you have gone the wrong way about knowing yourself, disclose nothing to the point. As an author of English prose, Newman has at least the negative virtue that, at a period when most writers were becoming cluttered in the Victorian manner, he wrote tolerably straightforwardly. But as an author of English verse he perhaps wrote more prosaically than any author of prose at any period.

Gerontius achieves what ought to have been the impossible: it is a longish narrative poem evoking the moment of death which never once provokes the reader's *timorem mortis*. Newman could probably have written a narrative poem describing sexual intercourse without once provoking the reader's eroticism. Perhaps a reader cannot sympathize with even a dying fellow-being who

45

urges himself on his deathbed 'Rouse thee, my fainting soul, and play the man'. Not for an instant can Newman strike into the bones that wild chill of mortality which the Latin liturgy can cast by an almost casual felicity like *quos contristat certa moriendi conditio*. Still less does Newman's demonic doggerel (unredeemed by Elgar's setting – it is Elgar who must be praised for transcending Newman) approach the divine doggerel of the *Dies Irae*. The *Dies Irae* lurches freely like a ship in a storm. Newman is clinging with a too naked awkwardness to the stanchions of his rhymes:

> Low-born clods
> Of brute earth,
> They aspire
> To become gods,
> By a new birth . . .

Yet the *Sanctus Fortis* section of *Gerontius* and the dedication – and perhaps even Newman's choice of title for his autobiography – suggest that any literary aptitude he had was for Latin rather than English. But in Latin, since the language was dead by the time his talent came to it, a quotation would gain a merit-mark as an elegance. Newman can't be credited with the line *De profundis oro te*. When he quotes and then freely translates, he can actually ruin the Latin. The priest at Gerontius's deathbed is given the lines

> Proficiscere, anima Christiana de hoc mundo!
> Go forth upon thy journey, Christian soul!
> Go from this world!

Presumably it was simply because he couldn't fit it in metrically that Newman had to weaken the awful unique occasion of going out of this world into the commonplace one of going forth upon a journey, until he could – too late – manoeuvre a literal translation into the next line. Presumably, too, it was technical maladroitness which drove him to such archaisms as 'nathless' and 'lets' in the sense of *prevents*.

The hymn for the 'choirs of angelicals' in *Gerontius* (or, to be exact, one of the five separate versions of it Newman provides in the course of the poem, though he in each case uses the same first verse) was adopted for use in religious worship not only by Catholics but by Anglicans. Aiming at poetry, Newman touched the lowest standard set by Hymns Ancient and Modern. (He was, while still an Anglican, the author of 'Lead, kindly light'.) In *Gerontius* he showed himself a poet whose notion of describing the sensations of a disembodied soul being transported by an angel was the passage

> . . . all around
> Over the surface of my subtle being,
> As though I were a sphere, and capable
> To be accosted thus, a uniform
> And gentle pressure tells me I am not
> Self-moving, but borne forward on my way.

NATHANIEL HAWTHORNE

The Scarlet Letter

' "It perplexes me," said Hilda thoughtfully, and shrinking a little. "Neither do I quite like to think about it." ' Although this passage comes from *The Marble Faun* it has its application in one's reaction to *The Scarlet Letter*. There is undoubtedly a sort of clumsy power in Hawthorne, blacker than he probably realized and one which he seems to have been unable artistically to control. The tone of *The Scarlet Letter* is so profoundly Puritanical that the book becomes a document in obsession; it is indeed something which one hardly wants to think about afterwards. The result is certainly not a novel, but a case history of hatred of the flesh. A vicious joy keeps repeating that the scarlet letter 'sears' the bosom of Hester Prynne: red-hot iron is the next stage of this sort of cruelty, in which the author half shares, while at times standing back and speaking distantly of the gloom of the period in which he has chosen to set his story.

It is an indication of Hawthorne's divided nature that he thinks in terms of guilt, sin and retribution for Hester Prynne but has a rather different fate in store for her 'demon offspring', little Pearl. The mother has been dragged through the book suffering every form of physical and mental agony (including the child's cruelty to her in recognizing her as a mother only when she wears the hateful scarlet A) but Pearl inherits the kingdom of the New World, and reaps a typical reward in becoming 'the richest heiress of her day'. If there is a lesson here, it is that there is material benefit eventually in being the child of an adulterous union.

For those who have committed adultery, however, there is nothing but agony. Nor does Hawthorne question the judgement of an intolerant Puritan society and the vile punishment it inflicts. He cannot dodge out of the issue by pretending that he is telling a story which requires no intrusion by the narrator – for the book is full of historical references ('At that epoch of pristine simplicity . . .') which betray the narrator's presence. It is therefore without irony, and with an effortless assumption of the standards of the Puritan figures enshrined in the book, that Hawthorne speaks of little Pearl as 'a lovely and immortal flower, (sprung) out of the rank luxuriance of a guilty passion'. The excess of condemnation in the very language suggests Hawthorne's unconscious preference for such a passion. He cannot condone it – still less is he capable of understanding it – but it excites his imagination. It has a luxuriance, according to him, which presumably is lacking to a conventional marriage. 'Questionable and troublesome enjoyments' was how Hawthorne once summed up his reaction to Rome; and the same judgement could equally apply to adultery.

The basic puritanism of *The Scarlet Letter* is the author's own. It is the reaction of the New England philistine—the same man who was shocked by nudity in antique Roman sculpture and disgusted by modern Roman behaviour. His mind was deliberately narrow, callow and frightened by prospects of pleasure, whether in art or life. He could not properly understand that the things he hated were things which dangerously appealed to him; in the violence of his rejection we have an indication of how intense was this appeal. Ambivalence is the mark of Hawthorne's own personal reaction to experience of every kind; but fear/love of the flesh is what underlies his character and his books. Secretly, and sometimes not so secretly, he is on the side of the persecutors of Hester Prynne. Women are dangerous, exotic creatures with white bosoms which can be cauterized only through the application of a scarlet A.

Hawthorne passes calmly under review every aspect of male intolerance, cruelty, emotional blackmail, repressed fears and secret emotions; aspects of life which are no doubt the more to be condoned as they lead to the accumulation of property and help to build a Godly, wealthy society. Women interrupt this harmony; they tempt men by beauty; they introduce sin into society. Hawthorne tacitly called up an army of male prejudice, while putting forward a vulgarly romantic idea of woman (or rather, Woman) which probably still remains the American dream. Passion and Affection – Hawthorne's capital letters – were no longer in Hester : 'Some attribute had departed from her, the permanence of which had been essential to keep her a woman.' But are passion and affection not essential to keep men as men? No. In Hawthorne's world they are too busy cutting up scarlet cloth so as to have plenty of letters ready to stick on the bosoms of the women they meet. And, very likely, that duty is the explanation which in America they give their wives for their habit of staring at other women's bosoms.

Aurora Leigh

Now that Mr Philip Toynbee has taken up the form, it is necessary to warn against the dangers of the novel-poem. Elizabeth Barrett Browning's *Aurora Leigh* can stand as the Most Awful Example. And attention ought to be drawn to *Aurora Leigh* for another reason. The letters of Elizabeth Barrett Browning are rightly admired. But her superb skill as a letter-writer may suggest to the unwary that she was equally talented as a poet. She was not. She ought to have been, but she was not. True, she thought of herself as a poet, she worked at her craft incessantly, she was devoted to what she imagined to be her calling. That she was mistaken is sad but irrefutable.

She went about it in such a humorlessly thorough manner that, if she had ever had any gift for writing verse, Miss Barrett would probably have suffocated it before she reached her teens by her incessant study of English and Greek prosody, and her so well-planned reading of both classical and modern literature. In her 'Glimpses into my own Life and Literary Character' written at the age of fourteen, she notes that her first poems were produced when she was four. So much for that other infant prodigy Mozart, who wrote nothing of any interest until he was six! Miss Barrett had also found time as a child to learn French, Italian, Greek and Latin, and she added several other languages while she was in her twenties. One pictures her dividing up her day into the reading hours and the writing hours. Her scholarship must have been impeccable, her erudition awesome. And yet what can possibly be said today in defence of her poetry? At her death she was widely regarded as one of the greatest poetesses of all time. Ruskin thought *Aurora Leigh* the greatest poem in the English language, 'unsurpassed by anything but Shakespeare – not surpassed by Shakespeare's sonnets'. George Eliot read *Aurora Leigh* at least three times, and knew of no book that gave her 'a deeper sense of communion with a large as well as beautiful mind'.

These eminent creatures, as well as the unspeakable Swinburne who was also a fervid admirer of the poem, were obviously dazzled by Elizabeth Barrett Browning's high-minded zeal, and by the sweetness of her personality. Today, gaping dry-eyed at the poems, we can hardly fail to notice her technical carelessness, her laziness and her inelegance, before turning away from her in distaste.

Aurora Leigh is like a libretto concocted from a George Sand novel. Mrs Browning, one knows, idolized George Sand ('the greatest female genius the world ever saw'), whose real name was Aurore Dupin. In fact she wrote an awful sonnet to George Sand who can hardly have cared for its opening line:

Thou large-brained woman and large-hearted man.

The plot of *Aurora Leigh* is incredible: the worst kind of sentimental Victoriana. Aurora refuses her cousin Romney, and embraces her muse. Romney decides to marry a poor seamstress who is stolen from him on the eve of their wedding by the horrid Lady Waldemar. Aurora later finds the seamstress in Paris: the poor girl has been raped, brothelized, drugged, and has had a child. Aurora takes the seamstress to Florence. Romney turns up. He has suffered misfortunes: for one thing, he is blind. Aurora and Romney are reunited.

Mrs Browning's narrative technique is as disordered as her plot; her way of writing about children is gruesome; Aurora is barely credible; the other characters hardly exist. The verse is, in general, virtually unreadable. At its worst of a dullness beyond belief, at its best it's undistinguished prose like this:

'Here's one, at least, who is good,' I sighed, and touched
Poor Marian's happy head, as doglike she,

Most passionately patient, waited on,
A-tremble for her turn of greeting words;
'I've sat a full hour with your Marian Erle,
And learnt the thing by heart, – and from my heart
Am therefore competent to give you thanks
For such a cousin.'

The Autocrat of the Breakfast Table

NATURALLY it was the breakfast table: his facetiousness, his bounce, his sententiousness accost you with precisely the effect of funny stories before 9 a.m. Not that Holmes runs much to *stories*; he's incapable of making even blunt points; he meanders, but at the pace of a torrent. In the paragraphs of classical allusion and quotation one might surmise a motive (showing off). Otherwise he seems to talk on and on through sheer wanton aggressiveness. The book might be someone's rough notes for a set of very full footnotes to something, what the something is being unguessable. Only Holmes would have actually supplied such a book with footnotes.

His manner suggests (can it be because he was a doctor?) that he's constantly pressed for time: 'Immense sensation at the table – sudden retirement of the angular female in oxydated bombazine. Movement of adhesion – as they say in the Chamber of Deputies – on the part of the young fellow they call John . . .' But what is he hurrying *for*? Perhaps to leave himself space for his sentimental passages: 'Ah, but I must not forget that dear little child I saw and heard in a French hospital. Between two and three years old . . . Lying in bed, patient, gentle. Rough students round her . . . but the child placid, perfectly still. I spoke to her, and the blessed little creature answered me in a voice of such heavenly sweetness, with the reedy thrill in it which you have heard in the thrush's even-song, that I seem to hear it at this moment, while I am writing, so many, many years afterwards.' No wonder Mark Twain used *The Autocrat of the Breakfast Table* as a 'courting-book' and that his wife kept it in a box 'with the love letters'. It might *be* Huck Finn's love-talk.

The Autocrat is in current print as a 'classic', in a paperback series professing to be 'a timeless treasury of the world's great writings'. Since none of Holmes's remarks has point or relevance in the internal context of his book, it is a kindness to apply one of them to his book's situation in a treasury of great writings: 'Literary life is full of curious phenomena. I don't know that there is anything more noticeable than what we may call *conventional reputations*. There is a tacit understanding in every community of men of letters that they will not disturb the popular fallacy respecting this or that electro-gilded celebrity.' It's time to admit the electro-gilt has worn away and there's nothing beneath.

Pickwick Papers

PERHAPS one ought not to attack so outrageously vulnerable a writer as Dickens by choosing what one considers to be one of his worst novels; but the fact is that *Pickwick Papers* is also one of his most popular. It is to some extent understandable that this should be so : it is easy to read, in the sense that one can pick it up, put it down, neglect it for some months and come back to it, secure in the knowledge that one is not thereby denying oneself any chance of appreciating its formal unity. It has none. It does not develop, it simply goes on. And on. But surely, one wonders, picaresque form does not necessarily preclude the possibility of the central character being acted upon, being influenced by events. True, it does not; nevertheless, Mr Pickwick remains as innocent at the end of *Pickwick Papers* as he was at the beginning. Dickens is working in an area so far removed from any conceivable kind of reality that it is hardly advantageous for us to think of Mr Pickwick as a character, except in the pejorative sense of one who is 'a card', 'a real character'. Mr Pickwick is both a 'real character', and the unrealest character of all.

There are two valid objections to this distressingly jolly charade of a novel. One can object both to the moral squalor of Dickens's intent and to the awfulness of his prose. *Pickwick Papers* appears to have been written in a series of jerkily spasmodic bouts of inane euphoria. For someone whose reputation rests in some degree on his progressive views (though even those tend to dissolve if one approaches them too closely), it is the most regressive and backward-looking of novels. Real existence – and not only the real existence of the time when Dickens was writing but also that of the past he writes about – is kept cheerily at bay. Cheerily. That's the adverb that immediately comes to mind in connection with Pickwick. Even the prison he finds himself in is a cheery sort of place where he is treated royally. Cheery and jolly. And this bogus jollity pervades the whole of *Pickwick Papers*. It is not, of course, only Mr Pickwick's jollity that is bogus, it is everything about him. He is simply a stock figure compounded of stock reactions to a series of stock incidents. Just as one can blame the ghastly Surtees and his horrid Jorrocks for having encouraged *Pickwick Papers* into existence, so one can blame *Pickwick* for virtually inventing not only the Christmas-card but the Christmas-card Christmas as well. The cosy family interiors, the crisp white snow glimpsed through the cottage windows, the stage-coach with its cheery coachmen, all are to be found in the glorious Ur-card that is *Pickwick*.

In addition to propagating this silly, childhood dream-world, Dickens in effect is telling us through *Pickwick* that the way to live our lives is dim-wittedly and self-indulgently, and that if we muddle through in this essentially selfish manner, all will come right in the end. Unfortunately the great novelist is mistaken, and, what's more, the series of jokes through which he conveys his advice, is dismally unfunny. Mr Pickwick's loathsome good cheer and innate snobbishness appear to have endeared him to the Victorian middle classes. His appeal today, however, is more probably to that elderly, self-educated working class to which Shaw addressed himself when he was young, and they and the twentieth century were younger. Does this perhaps explain why several modern novelists of working-class origin tend to write the way Mr Pickwick talked?

The huge supply of characters in *Pickwick* is impressive until one notices that they are really all alike. Dickens goes to great lengths to describe their physical appearance in a vain attempt to persuade one that they are different. They may *look* different, but their gestures and attitudes are remarkably alike. Dickens cannot create the illusion of reality, only the reality of quaintness. No, not even that: although he continually insists on the quaintness of his characters, we as often as not remain unconvinced. These caricatures come from nowhere, live nowhere. Alfred Jingle Esq. actually admits to living at 'No Hall, Nowhere', and in his schizoid utterance one has the whole boring length of *Pickwick Papers* in microcosm.

Dickens's essentially feudal attitude to society is revealed in the Pickwick-Sam Weller relationship, and his absurd yearning for an impossibly unreal past permeates almost every sentence of *Pickwick*. What many people respond to in this book is its association with nostalgia for childhood, for a time when one's own actions were allowed to be as irresponsible as those of Mr Pickwick. It is, at any rate, more easily understandable that readers should enjoy their own harmless fantasy than that they should take delight in the cringing prose style, the long-winded asides, the vomit-making pathos and appeals to mindless sentimentality which are what one finds on the printed page. Far better to read between the lines, since the language actually on the lines is at worst that of a barn-storming trickster, at best that of an anonymous syndicate. This poetaster of cosiness and smug banality has little to offer today. *Pickwick Papers*, never a work of art, hasn't even managed to succeed as good, clean fun.

The Warden

It is possible that the entire literary career of Anthony Trollope is an act of expiation for the unseemliness of his surname. (His method of work certainly suggests expiation rather than inspiration.) In a sense, there is nothing wrong with Trollope – but he carries it to the point where that is what is wrong with him. He is always in perfect good taste.

That cannot be blamed on his period. Both Thackeray and Dickens were – sometimes distressingly, sometimes superbly – vulgar. Trollope avoided their excesses and also (with, one feels, even more of a shudder) their excess of genius. He treads the *via media* with what might pass for an eighteenth-century dislike of enthusiasm, except that in Trollope the dislike is not backed up by a classical and penetrating intellect, with the result that the *via media* turns out to be a suburban garden path. Indeed, Trollope *is* that nice, maundering spinster lady with a poke bonnet and a taste for cottagey gardens whom superficial readers *thought* they had got hold of when they had in fact got hold of the morally sabre-toothed Jane Austen.

Trollope's plots are as shamelessly wrenched as Dickens's but Trollope unfairly escapes the accusation of melodrama by confining them to domestic and miniaturistic settings. He dodges the accusation of sentimentality by squeezing instead of jerking his tears. By writing a plainish, porridge-like prose, he *seems* to avoid the crockets of Victorian gothic: but they're there all the same – 'And did she find these details tedious? Oh, no – she encouraged him to dilate on every feeling he expressed . . .' 'Dear ladies, you are right as to your appreciation of the circumstances, but very wrong as to Miss Harding's character.' Likewise he *seems* not to caricature his characters; but the broadness of his character-drawing is obscured by the small proportion he gives of dialogue to narrative. What dialogue there is belongs to the un-telling, repetitively naturalistic type, and his narrative manner is condescending ('Mr Chadwick had just come from London and was therefore known to be the bearer of important news') though the condescension is carefully offered only from medium height.

Significantly, and to the final exoneration of his period, although Trollope's wholesale production of lavender water found some market during his lifetime, it was not until the 1939–45 war that he became a popular (indeed, a paperback) novelist. Perhaps it was then that the English middle classes discovered that Jane Austen was not what they had supposed and took to Trollope in her place, hoping to rebut through him the threat extended by bombs, and still more by evacuees, to the whole Thames valley gamut of English 'good taste' – the Wedgwood Jasper Ware, the gilt-framed prints of Redouté roses on the satin-striped walls, the place-mats after the 'Cries of London' series – whereby the British Bourgeoisie demonstrates to its neighbour that it is cultivated, without having to undergo the martyrdom of being actually and emotionally moved by works of art.

Jane Eyre

Jane Eyre is blatantly such stuff as daydreams are made on – every bit as blatantly as, say, *Hadrian VII*. Charlotte Brontë belongs somewhere near Corvo in the sweetmeat shop, though on a broader and more accessible shelf. Whereas reading *Hadrian VII* is like making oneself delicately queasy on halva, reading *Jane Eyre* is like gobbling a jar-full of schoolgirl stickjaw. So naive a work, even though it is likely to give one a pain in the belly, provokes no serious quarrel in its own right. One can take issue only with the Eng. Lit. doctors who, though undeceived by Corvo's immeasurably greater learning and self-consciousness, have been fooled by *Jane Eyre*'s emotional pretensions and have put the stout old jar of toffee on display in the china cabinet. There *Jane Eyre* still stands – newly issued, indeed, in a paperback series of 'the literary masterpieces which have appeared in the English language since the fifteenth century'. And this edition is equipped with an introduction claiming 'Where Charlotte Brontë is so superior to Dickens is in her creation of positives' and 'even the best part' (sc. of *The Mill on the Floss*), 'the study of the child and schoolgirl, is immensely inferior in power and achievement to the corresponding first two sections of *Jane Eyre*'.

To be precise, *Jane Eyre* is such stuff as two daydreams are made on. The first concerns the put-upon child who eventually gets her own back on everyone. The orphaned and impoverished Jane Eyre comes into her £20,000 much as the rejected and persecuted George Arthur Rose comes into the papacy; and both thereupon behave with the saintly magnanimity which expert daydreamers know to be so much sweeter than revenge in its cruder form.

Jane, however, is not quite so expert as George Arthur. Less self-controlled, she cannot refrain from leaking little dribbles of her triumph in advance. Cruelly and unjustly punished by the adults, she or her creator can't wait till she becomes adult herself; the infant Jane must enjoy her daydream vindication there and then : she must fall grievously ill on the spot and as a direct result of adult unkindness, the doctor must be called and the adults must be shown up and shamed in his sight.

Time and again this impatience to anticipate the daydream dénouement spoils the dramatic effect. Jane Eyre as narrator vigorously, if not subtly, builds up the character of Mr Brocklehurst through his own dialogue. 'Oh, shocking!' he exclaims when he learns of Jane's indifference to the Psalms. 'I have a little boy, younger than you, who knows six Psalms by heart : and when you ask him which he would rather have, a gingerbread-nut to eat, or a verse of a Psalm to learn, he says : "Oh! the verse of a Psalm! angels sing Psalms", says he.' So far so good, if crude; and the crudity may be justified as straight reporting. But the narrator is then betrayed by her own indignation. She cannot wait to show Mr Brocklehurst for an ass by oblique methods. She insists he condemn himself on the spot and out of his own mouth; and she makes him continue his speech not merely with an implausibly naked self-revelation but in the very sardonic accents that would be used by, and could be used only by, a third person commenting adversely on him. Mr Brocklehurst goes on to relate that his little boy 'then gets two nuts in recompense for his infant piety'. The error is repeated when Mr Brocklehurst visits the school where Jane is now a pupil. Mr Brocklehurst is in the act of declaiming that the pupils must be taught 'to clothe themselves with shamefacedness and sobriety, not with braided hair and costly apparel' when the impatient narrator has him interrupted by the entrance of his own wife and daughters 'splendidly attired in velvet, silk, and furs'. An ironist makes his readers hold their breath until the echo is returned. Charlotte Brontë dissipates what might have been irony in mere invective.

The second daydream in *Jane Eyre* is sexual and belongs to a different period of the daydreamer's life. Some of the awkwardness of patching the two ages and the two fantasies together is probably reflected in the clumsy bridge-passage that begins Chapter 10 of the novel (whose sub-title is 'an autobiography') : 'Hitherto I have recorded in detail the events of my insignificant existence : to the first ten years of my life I have given almost as many chapters. But this is not to be a regular autobiography ... I now pass a space of eight years almost in silence.' The space turns Jane into an adult and involves her in a sado-masochistic relation with Mr Rochester, whom she, as a governess in his employ, addresses as 'sir' and lovingly thinks of as her 'Master' but whom, while they are engaged to be married, she disciplines quite as though she were *his* governess : 'I assured him I was naturally hard – very flinty ... He fretted, pished and pshawed. "Very good", I thought : "you may fume and fidget as you please; but this is the best plan to pursue with you, I am certain." '

But not all this second fantasy belongs to adult life. Its core is the Oedipus situation, with Mr Rochester playing father-figure. The marriage of Jane Eyre and Mr Rochester is foiled at the very altar by the impediment which prevents every little girl from marrying her father, namely that he is married already. (Such a tiresome impediment, mama – mad, of course, and dangerously incendiary.) Mrs Q. D. Leavis, the author of that introduction which asserts *Jane Eyre*'s superiority to Dickens and George Eliot, records that 'Mr Rochester has been the object of a good deal of derision' and grants 'Unfortunately, unlike Jane Austen, who was immune to the vulgarization of the Romantic movement represented by Byronism, the Brontës' daydreams had clearly been formed on Byronic lines.' (If Mrs Leavis's syntax is to be taken seriously, she is stating that Jane Austen was not formed on Byronic lines, but it may be safer to guess she intends to speak of Jane Austen's daydreams.) It is more to the point, however, that Charlotte Brontë's daydreams had clearly been formed by the Oedipal stress. The little girl can escape the guilt of her erotic relation to her father if her father is castrated : before Jane Eyre can marry her father-figure, he is mutilated in the fire that destroys his house. He loses an arm and almost all his sight – an emphatic symbolic castration, betokened twice over, by the direct

67

loss of a limb and by the blinding that is the symbol used in the Oedipus story itself. (Mr Rochester is phallicized and castrated yet again by being likened to a tree – whose blasting by lightning forecasts, according to Mrs Leavis, his mutilation.) Charlotte Brontë's choice of mutilations was, perhaps, influenced also by an historical example. The sightless and armless Mr Rochester seems to be formed on the lines less of the clubfooted Lord Byron than of the war-wounded Lord Nelson (duke, of course, of Brontë).

Jane Eyre essentially recites these two fantasies one after the other, with only a cursory gesture towards slotting the end of the first into the working-out of the second. Mrs Leavis quotes Lord David Cecil's finding that Charlotte Brontë 'has no gift of form' and rebuts it with (i) 'This reaction to *Jane Eyre* seems to me to show an inability to read', and (ii) the claim that the book sticks to its theme, that 'the theme has, very properly, dictated the form' and that the theme is 'an exploration of how a woman comes to maturity in the world of the writer's youth' – an account of it which must surely either make the first nine chapters super-fluous to the form or show up the eight-year gap as a flaw in the form supposedly dictated by the theme.

The most Charlotte Brontë does to unite the two fantasies is to withold the final vindication of the child, the £20,000, until after the adolescent with her Oedipus fixation has been foiled in her first attempt to marry Mr Rochester. This involves her, however, in perhaps the most outrageous coincidence in the re-pertory of melodramatic plot making. Running away from bigamy, Jane stumbles at random about the English countryside until, on the point of death, she begs shelter, and is received in and succoured. Presently her helpers turn out to be her unknown cousins. (They are newly disappointed of a legacy; the person it has gone to instead is Jane.)

When her male cousin proposes marriage to her, Jane runs away again, this time back to Mr Rochester. By perhaps the most outrageous coincidence in the repertory of happy endings, the fire which, by maiming him, has removed the unconscious psychological impediment to their marriage, has conveniently destroyed also the legal impediment, his wife.

As well as defying the laws of chance, *Jane Eyre* gives a good tossing to the laws of nature by way of much symbolic weather and a premonitory dream or two, and at last finally infringes nature with a supernatural event. Tempted to marry her cousin, Jane hears a disembodied voice cry 'Jane! Jane!' and shouts back 'I am coming! Wait for me! . . . Where are you?' She then sets off to find where he (Mr Rochester, of course) is. He has been a thirty-six-hour coach journey distant from her all along. Yet, he relates to her when they meet, 'As I exclaimed, "Jane! Jane! Jane!" a voice – I cannot tell whence the voice came, but I know whose voice it was – replied "I am coming; wait for me"; and a moment after, went whispering on the wind the words, "Where are you?" ' As narrator, Jane Eyre solemnly adds 'Reader, it was on Monday night – near midnight – that I too had received the mysterious summons; those were the very words . . .', etc.

Mrs Leavis remarks 'The considerable element in the novel of folk-lore, fairy-tale, the supernatural, and the uncanny was deeply rooted in local beliefs, and supplied in the home by their devoted Tabby' (the Brontës' servant). But Mrs Leavis adds 'Of course, no amount of pointing to sources affects the conclusion that Charlotte Brontë . . . was a splendidly original artist.' Well: perhaps the whisper on the wind at midnight on Monday is to be explained by Tabby and splendid originality. Or perhaps Charlotte Brontë had simply read this bit of *Moll Flanders*: 'I fell into a vehement fit of crying, every now and then calling him by his name . . . "O Jemmy!" said I, "come back, come back". . . . thus I passed the afternoon, till about seven o'clock . . . when, to my unspeakable surprise, he comes back . . . I told him . . . how loud I had called upon him . . . He told me he heard me very plain upon Delamere Forest, at a place about twelve miles off . . . "Why", said I, "what did I say?" – for I had not named the words to him. "You called aloud", says he, "and said, 'O Jemmy! O Jemmy! come back, come back.' " '

Wuthering Heights

Wuthering Heights will wash as a psychological–historical curio or as high old rumbustious nonsense, but not as a great novel.

The truth is that it's the result of Emily Brontë's taking with hysterical seriousness the gothic novels Jane Austen sent up. *Wuthering Heights* is literally a ghost story, and it creaks with the gothic ghost story's semi-literate, ball-and-chain-dragging language : 'I had no desire to aggravate his impatience, previous to inspecting the penetralium.'

How this farrago has imposed on the critics is not hard to explain. 'Wuthering Heights is the name of Mr Heathcliff's dwelling. "Wuthering" being a significant provincial adjective, descriptive of the atmospheric tumult to which its station is exposed in stormy weather.' Naturally the English have been gulled into supposing it a great book when it makes so much of the weather. Playing more shamelessly than any other work of fiction on the pathetic fallacy, it invites English readers to excuse the lack of psychological coherence and emotional truth in its characters by confusing those characters with elemental forces; and one critic has obediently divided the characters into 'children of storm' and 'children of calm', while another sees Catherine and Heathcliff as 'portions of the flux of nature'.

However, the elemental force which really inspires *Wuthering Heights* is more on the lines of those poltergeists which are said to attach themselves to sexually disturbed adolescents. What sort of book it really is it betrays through its hero, that 'dark skinned gypsy' who is none the less 'in aspect, in dress, and manners a gentleman . . . not looking amiss with his negligence, because he has an erect and handsome figure, and rather morose'. Ultimately derived, no doubt, from Satan by way of Lord Byron, Heathcliff foreshadows uncountable Sheiks and Men in Grey; and *Wuthering Heights* itself is both the first and the meatiest morsel in the long, broad tradition of melodramatic daydreams concocted often by, and always to satisfy the appetites of, women wailing for their demon lovers.

NOW VACANT. Gent's dwelling, lofty station, exten. views. Heavy leaded casement windows, many lacking glass. No mod. con. Wood fires throughout. Penetralium or wd make rumpus room. Suit single lady.

Moby Dick or The White Whale

So they constructed a synthetic one for the film? But only by a grievous misjudgement did the one in the book ever pass for genuine. Even on the level of natural-historical observation Moby Dick isn't a true whale. 'Be it known,' writes the narrator, 'that, waiving all argument, I take the good old-fashioned ground that the whale is a fish' – a wrong guess which he can't even square with his own apprehension of the facts, since he later writes of 'nursing mothers' among whales. Still less is Moby Dick the organic product of a true imagination. He's a mere inflated pretend-whale, inflated by the sheer wish that American literature should run to profundity.

The humblest claim made for Melville by his idolators is that he spins a good yarn : and he belies even that. Three-quarters of *Moby Dick* is a monument to Melville's inability to get down to telling his story at all. A hundred or so chapters elapse in dissertations, digressions, moralizings, symbolizings and chunks quoted from dictionaries and encyclopaedias before the narrative proper starts; and when it does, it turns out to be a slight little anecdote which comes too quickly and goes for almost nothing. Conrad, with all his technical cunning, would have been hard put to it to elaborate a short story out of the captain who, having lost a leg to the unique albino whale, seeks vengeance so monomaniacally and so recklessly as to lose his own life, his crew's and his ship. Melville is simply not up to the swift graphic narrative required by the externals of the tale. He muddies the action alternately with bathos and with would-be poeticisms and inversions: '. . . as if sucked into a morass, Moby Dick sideways writhed'; 'three of the oarsmen – who foreknew not the precise instant of the dart, and were therefore unprepared for its effects – these were flung out'. The internals, the psychology, Melville cannot even make a put at, since he cannot create Captain Ahab's obsession but can only refer to it. Indeed, the whole of *Moby Dick* is a gigantic memorandum, to the effect 'What a story this would make, if told by someone who knew how to tell stories'. Even that is a mis-estimate: it wouldn't.

Melville is not a novelist: he is an annotator and labeller. Throughout the superfluous hundred chapters before he appears, the white whale's shadow is cast at the reader in advance; and Melville, who is basically a lantern-lecturer (of the kind whose own chiaroscuro mannerisms provoke audiences to say 'What an actor he'd make' – again a mis-estimate: he wouldn't), constantly labels – but never *makes* – the shadow 'portentous'. Ishmael (that most confusing of narrators, since he narrates information he can't, within the terms of his own narrative, have possessed) hasn't so much as set foot on a whaler when he first calls a whale 'a portentous and mysterious monster'. In a sailors' lodging house he sees a painting of a whale which he twice in a paragraph describes as 'portentous'. By the time he's on board, even the appetites of the ship's company strike him as 'portentous'. The only item in the book that might be truly labelled portentous is Ishmael's own narrative manner. 'All these things are not without their meanings', he portentously says – without, however, saying what the meanings are, unless they lurk in the intellectual pretentiousness whereby he speaks of two dead whales' heads as 'Locke's head' and 'Kant's'. Sharks eating whales' corpses are pronounced by Ishmael 'a part of the universal problem of all things'. What, however, isn't?

Many novelists have tried to anticipate the critic's task by writing both narrative and a commentary alongside it pointing out the deeper beauties, profundities and significances of the narrative. Melville alone has supplied the commentary without supplying the narrative.

Moby Dick is shadow play by a Victorian-Gothic whale of papier-mâché. When he spouts, up comes a cacophonous false rhetoric ('meads and glades so eternally vernal that . . .'). When he sports, he is grotesque in his whimsy ('as when the red-cheeked, dancing girls, April and May, trip home'), obese in his facetiousness ('he was stopped on the way by a portly Sperm Whale, that begged a few moments' confidential business with him') and ungainly in his sprightliness ('The act of paying is perhaps the most uncomfortable infliction that the two orchard thieves entailed upon us'). He's worst of all when he fumbles for a metaphysical conceit in which to embody an emotional moment: 'Their hands met; their eyes fastened; Starbuck's tears the glue.'

Distended with hot air himself, Melville's whale can beget no progeny except wind eggs. One of them contained just life enough to hatch into the crocodile in *Peter Pan*. Otherwise, the whale is father to nothing but the dozens of novels which, with only the proper name altered, have repeated his burly opening sentence, 'Call me Ishmael', and the misconceptions that (*a*) the Great American Novel can be written by thinking about writing it instead of thinking about whatever it is about, (*b*) that it must be about brutality to animals, and (*c*) that brutality to animals, if pursued by men whose tears are the glue which fasten their eyes to the eyes of their fellow men, is manly and portentous. (Where did all the great white whales go? They went Hemingway.) *Moby Dick* is American literature's pseudo-founding-father, its false prophet in fake biblical prose, its Reproduction Antique ancient monument. American literature is now old enough and good enough to sell off the great white elephant.

Leaves of Grass

WHAT is one to say of this garrulous old bore? His style is nothing more than a full-throated 'Yippee!' and, in this instance, *le style* is undoubtedly *l'homme*.

In common with a significantly large proportion of American writers, he really hates the art of writing. There is something suspect about literature, he feels. It's an understandable pastime for those oppressed Europeans, but it shouldn't be necessary in God's own country. 'The trouble is,' he announced towards the end of his life, 'that writers are too damned literary.'

'Damned,' used in that sense, is a favourite expression of the American writer. It emphasizes his demotic aspect, his down-to-earth, commonsensical undamned and unliterary ordinariness. And Whitman is the American author *par excellence*.

As he sings or rather roars at the top of his voice the body electric, piling catalogue upon catalogue:

Mouth, tongue, lips, teeth, roof of the mouth and the jaw
  hinges,
Nose, nostrils of the nose, and the partition,
Cheeks, temples, forehead, chin, throat, back of the neck,
  neck-slue,
Strong shoulders, manly beard, scapula, hind-shoulders, and
  the ample side-round of the chest,
Upper-arm, armpit, elbow-socket, lower arm, arm sinews,
  arm-bones,

> Wrist and wrist-joints, hand, palm knuckles, thumb, fore-
>   finger, finger joints, finger nails,
> Broad breast-front, curling hair of the breast, breast-bone,
>   breast-side,
> Ribs, belly, backbone, joints of the backbone,
> Hips, hip-sockets, hip-strength, inward and outward round,
>   man-balls, man-root,
> Strong set of thighs, well-carrying the trunk above,
> Leg-fibres, knee, knee-pan, upper-leg, under-leg,
> Ankles, instep, foot-ball, toes, toe-joints, the heel;

one can only flinch, and note hurriedly that this sort of thing is not even the bad verse for which he is famous. It is quite simply non-verse. Whitman's poetic personality does not merely verge on caricature, it topples riotously over the edge. It is astonishing that several generations of critics have managed to accept this verbal masturbation as poetry.

Whitman's so-called poetry ranges from a simpleton's idea of Shakespeare and the purpler passages of the Bible to sheer semi-literate sludge. His subject is everything, nothing. His principal interest, though he hardly realizes the fact seriously, is sex; but he is incredibly prissy about it. His attitude is that of the timidly fascinated virgin. In a post-Freudian age, he would probably not have written at all : one hopes he would, at any rate, have spent less time being fascinated with and repelled by his homo-sexuality, and more time enjoying himself in the practice of it. For all his loudly proclaimed earthiness, his language continually shies away from the realities of feeling, and from what he ob-viously considers to be coarse. Not only has he no sexual contact with anyone but himself, he equally lacks emotional and mental contact with the outside world. When a lady who had read *Leaves of Grass* took him at his word and wrote to the poet in his own language, 'My womb is clean and pure. It is ready for thy child my love. Angels guard the vestibule until thou comest to deposit our and the world's precious treasure', poor Walt took fright. Even the iceman cometh, but Whitman cometh not, except into his own (so to speak).

This banal and sententious old fraud has a certain validity and stature as a comic figure, but as the great sexual emancipator he hardly begins to exist. He couldn't bring himself to speak of a venereal disease other than as 'the bad disorder'. And when he apostrophizes his 'camerado close' in the mawkish, autoerotic daydream, 'Premonition',

> O camerado close! O you and me at last, and us two only.
> O a word to clear one's path ahead endlessly!
> O something ecstatic and undemonstrable! O music wild!
> O now I triumph – and you shall also;
> O hand in hand – O wholesome pleasure – O one more desirer and lover!
> O to haste firm holding – to haste, haste on with me.

the reader can be certain of two things: that the 'wholesome pleasure' Walt deeply and secretly desires is plain, unadultered sex which he can never consciously bring himself to admit as wholesome; and that if the camerado had ever responded by laying a hand on the poet's Walt-celebrated penis, Walt would have uttered a squawk of terror, gathered up his skirts and fled.

> Mannahatta a-march – and it's O to sing it well!
> It's O for a manly life in the camp.

Rather a camp life in the men, as Miss Mae West would have pointed out.

Footnote: Was it not Walt who posed for a photograph of himself with a butterfly lovingly fluttering on his index finger? The butterfly was discovered to be a dead one, mounted on a ring the poet was wearing.

There is more life in that dead butterfly than in Walt's 'pomes'.

Alice's Adventures in Wonderland

THE Reverend Charles Lutwidge Dodgson, alias Lewis Carroll, was, as we all know, a very ordinary Victorian clergyman. That is, he was kinky about little girls, and he was an extremely dull, humourless man. To make matters worse, he lectured in Mathematics at Christ Church, Oxford, for over a quarter of a century. Yet he produced, in addition to the usual boring treatises, a number of books for children, two of which – *Alice's Adventures in Wonderland* and *Through the Looking Glass* – have come to be regarded as classics of their kind. He was nowhere near as gifted as Edward Lear, whose nonsense verses make Carroll's efforts in this direction appear very laboured, but he has somehow managed to survive in the popular imagination in a way that Lear has not. *Through the Looking Glass*, the sequel to *Alice*, is quite amusing, though children don't usually find it so. But *Alice*, by far the more discussed and highly regarded of the two books, is a comparatively laboured affair.

Dodgson invented mathematical problems in order to occupy the mind and divert it from 'the unholy thoughts which torture with their hateful presence the fancy that would fain be pure': reading *Alice* one cannot avoid the uncomfortable feeling that Carroll improvised it somewhat abstractedly in order to banish impure thoughts both from his own mind and from Alice Liddell's. The fantasy is anything but free-ranging: it lurches from one laboured situation to the next. Do children believe

Alice's adventures in the way that children *do* believe the absurd and the fanciful? They do not. There is something not quite right about it all. The nice gentleman telling the tale is making it up too glibly, too arbitrarily. His mind is on something else : something impure, no doubt.

The imagination that contrived the adventures of Alice is a tired imagination. There are, of course, occasional felicities in the book; but the Mad Hatter is not mad enough, the White Rabbit is too frantically dull, and the Reverend Dodgson's frequent parentheses continually destroy what atmosphere there is. In short, Alice does not really descend into Wonderland, she just doesn't get off the ground at all. Children aren't fond of the book, and adults either forget that as children they did not like it, or pretend that they did. After all it's such a nice, wholesome, dull book.

Tom Brown's Schooldays

To say so may be tautologous, but Thomas Hughes is really a nineteenth-century Kingsley Amis. The two novelists share a splendid insularity of thought and manner, and an extraordinary infelicity of expression. Hughes is, perhaps marginally the more literate of the two, but on the other hand his novels are of a far greater length. The first thing to be said about *Tom Brown's Schooldays* is that it is three or four times as long as it has any right to be, due in great part to the author's irritating habit of interrupting his deadly tale to harangue the reader with his views on almost any subject that creeps into his reactionary and conventional mind. One such subject is the wretched habit of 'young England' of gallivanting around the Continent instead of staying decently at home. And, not content with being a xenophobe, Hughes is a vile old snob as well. The well-bred Tom is constantly being contrasted with the quaint yokels to whom he is required to set an example. Tom Brown is, not surprisingly, an overwhelmingly priggish youngster whose character degenerates year by year at Rugby School until he leaves it a well turned-out, brainwashed automaton. The process by which this is achieved is described by the author in terms of evident approval. Doubtless one should take the sophisticated view of *Tom Brown's Schooldays* – that it is a damning indictment of the English public-school system. But though this may be the only possible reading to give it today, those who uphold it as 'the finest novel of school-life that we have' probably don't see it in that light.

Life at Rugby is grim. According to Hughes, however, the habit of 'silent endurance' is dear to every Englishman, and is no doubt largely responsible for English superiority over other nations. The grotesque 'character-building' that Dr Arnold and his staff of hypocrites and bullies indulge in is quite blatantly ruinous to character. Yet the entire rigmarole is gushed over and lauded by Hughes: the games cult, for instance. When the school is paying football, attendance at the match by non-performers is not made compulsory because it's unthinkable that anyone should be intelligent enough to avoid the match in favour of a good book, or a quiet snooze, or a private fumble with a chum in a deserted dorm. 'They trust to our honour,' one of the ghastly good boys tells Tom. 'They know very well that no School-house boy would cut the match. If he did, we'd very soon cut him, I can tell you.' That by the way is a fair sample of the way the Rugby inmates talk to each other: in other words, Hughes does not have much of an ear for dialogue.

Hughes does have, and in abundance, a stomach for the most dangerous sentimentality about the School. Not only does he allow his characters to indulge themselves in it unashamedly, he even interrupts them to add his own voice. Stand up for your own old school, he exhorts us. Knock the fellow down who says his is better. The logical extension of following this advice is civil war; but perhaps Hughes means us to stop short of that. Of course he does. Life is a great quad in which we must all struggle, one against the other; but a moment always comes when the master calls a halt, shamefacedly we stop fighting, shake hands with one another and swear eternal friendship.

Usually, even from the worst of school stories, there is some slight pornographic enjoyment to be derived. It should be made clear that there's no good clean fun of this kind to be had with *Tom Brown*. Christ-like sublimation is the order of the day. In fact Christ enters the story quite early on, and is rarely absent from it thereafter. Of the first sermon that Tom hears Dr Arnold deliver, 'more worthy pens than mine have described that scene' says Hughes. And we believe him. 'The tall gallant form, the kindling eye, the voice, now soft as the low notes of a flute, now clear and stirring as the call of the light infantry bugle.' There are pages more of this kind of thing: fortunately nowhere is there any indication of what the tall, gallant Doctor actually said.

Hughes doesn't really approve of bullies, but they're necessary to him because he likes thrashing, so needs bullies to thrash. The bullies, of course, enjoy it. After one boy has had a 'good sound thrashing', Hughes leaps, momentarily, into the future to tell us that 'years afterwards that boy sought out Holmes and thanked him, saying it had been the kindest act which had ever been done upon him'. What, dare one ask, were the others? It's all very well for this happy masochist to declare himself satisfied : the reader remains unsatisfied, since Hughes's description of the 'good sound thrashing' is as lacking in detail as his account of Arnold's sermon.

No, there's no sex at Rugby, apart from the author's one reference in a footnote to 'many noble friendships between big and little boys'. 'Thank goodness no big fellow ever took to petting me,' says Tom, and it does seem only too likely that the big fellows were able to find metal more attractive than prissy little Tom Brown.

Like most religious fanatics, Hughes has more than a streak of belligerence in his make-up. He despises Quaker pacifism, and goes out of his way to tell us so. He'd rather, he says, see people fighting the wrong people and the wrong things, than have no fight in them. What with the fighting, and the taking of Communion, and the praying in the dorm, and Tom's proselytizing zeal ('Only there's some great dark strong power, which is crushing you and everybody else. That's what Christ conquered and we've got to fight'), and his apotheosis at Arnold's tomb, the atmosphere is pretty soggily pre-Raphaelite.

Tom Brown's Schooldays is really a remarkable book : remarkable for the viciousness of its moral attitudes, and the numbing dullness with which these attitudes are expressed.

The Golden Treasury

FRANCIS PALGRAVE has made a name by picking an anthology of other men's flowers, which he was fully entitled to do. But it was going a dangerous step further when conceit allowed him to give his choice its golden adjective of approval and add 'of the best songs and lyrical poems in the English language'. In vain did he dedicate the result to Tennyson, the Poet Laureate, and try to blame the whole thing on the geography of Wales: 'Your encouragement given while traversing the wild scenery of Treryn Dinas, led me to begin the work.'

Palgrave's sins of omission are famous, shameless and ludicrous. In themselves they utterly flaw the value of his absurd claim. The absence of any line by Donne, the failure to include Marvell's *Ode to his Coy Mistress*, the inability to suggest Pope's quality... these are merely the opening shots which should riddle the wretched boat's mean sail. They would indeed be effective ammunition, were it not that the cargo is itself further ammunition; few vaunted treasures have ever held as much dross as Palgrave managed to pack on board – almost enough to sink the unsinkable vessel of English literature. Whether Tennyson or the scenery of Treryn Dinas exercised a malign influence it is now impossible to say. The culprit must remain the only compiler, whose concept of the best in English lyrical poetry is largely mediocre, unnecessarily conventional, and judged always by the standards not of inspiration but of the stuffiest and dreariest mid-Victorian drawing-room. How far his conventional reactions and consistent prudery were unnecessary is shown by the fact that even in the suffocating respectability of Ruskin's childhood home Byron's *Don Juan* was approved reading. Yet Palgrave's compilation goes staggering on, into edition after edition, with desperate repairs being done to the rear of the volume, packing in those living poets Palgrave discreetly excluded. Somebody has even put in a poem by Oliver Wendell Holmes (q.v.) which is in itself a disgraceful plagiarism of Wordsworth, as well as a sickening piece of maundering rubbish in its own right. No doubt Palgrave would have approved; and juxtaposed to the verse by Scott, Cibber, Rogers and Barbauld, O. W. Holmes is well situated.

Some wonder might be felt on considering where Palgrave found the poets he got out for drawing-room inspection. It may be suspected that they were already in the drawing-room and he did no more than give them a dusting and put them back in deeper respectability on the fringed and crowded mantelshelf. It is not until the third book – when we immediately encounter T. Gray (q.v.) – that Palgrave has good opportunities to fall among banality. This is indeed something of a testing point, though it could be anticipated that Palgrave (who had picked out just a few airy trifles among metaphysical poets) would seize on the more romantic and ballad-style aspects of the eighteenth century. Gray's *The Bard* thus appears in full, giving ample opportunity for one to see that it is among the worst poems in the English language. A weakness for Scottish dialect presumably accounts for something by someone called 'R. Graham of Gartmore' – making his first and last appearance in our literature. Utterly conventional and slightly out of date taste appears to account for another 'poet', Samuel Rogers, who has not kept his reputation. A great deal more Gray, interspersed with Collins, is followed soon after by yet another work by the poet Rogers – this one of quite remarkable triteness and implausibility. Is English literature really reduced to the lyrical poems of this person? They are the more cruelly revealed in their insipid stiffness by Palgrave's liberal representation of Burns. Perhaps this is an accident occasioned by Burns' use of dialect, because Palgrave's own taste soon has him picking out for the golden seal of approval poems by Sewell, Barbauld, H. Coleridge and J. Campbell (note the initials). If these are the great lights of English lyrical poetry, it is hardly surprising that Scott and Southey have managed to creep into the company; their jog-trot rhymes and commonplace reflections are joined by the voice of Thomas Campbell, whose *Lord Ullin's Daughter* becomes, by comparison, a superb piece of poetry as well as the fine ballad it undoubtedly is.

The Golden Treasury is an insult to English literature, not merely emasculated but misrepresented by Palgrave. It is difficult to devise a punishment to fit his shabby-genteel crime. Perhaps it should start with his having to write out a hundred times that lyric which begins:

Go and catch a falling star,
Get with child a mandrake root . . .

Lorna Doone

MANY of us who have not met Clara Vaughan, Alice Lorraine, Erema or Mary Anerley have been forced into acquaintance with their sister Lorna Doone. She is the classic one who made it, while Blackmore's other girls seem to have been left as wall-flowers in the Eng. Lit. dance, destined to wither without academic partners. It is not, however, *their* fate which is unjust, but hers. She lingers on – no longer fresh or appealing – a ghost in the ballroom of Victorian novels. Appearing in the year (1869) the Suez Canal was opened, she was probably already rather an old-fashioned thing, with ample skirts and Biblical manners (all stiff inverted sentences and cloudy moralizing). Blackmore destroyed verisimilitude and virtually created boredom by making his narrator John Ridd a plain man of great strength and effort-less narcissism. When Ridd confronts his enemy it is natural for him to think the man frightened by 'my stern blue eyes'; and though the story purports to be about his love for Lorna Doone it is really one long ogling of his own muscles in an Old Testa-ment mirror (despite a protest of being shy of looking-glasses) : 'it is almost beyond me to forbear saying that I must have looked very pleasing'. As well as crashing and smashing around Exmoor, with brief interludes of being in London on the King's business, John Ridd has moments of love-making which are conceived equally in terms of coy self-satisfaction : 'my great hand was creeping in a manner not to be imagined, and far less explained, toward the lithesome, wholesome curving underneath her mantle-fold . . .'

Not even the mawkish love passages are funny enough to disturb the deep tedium of the Exmoor landscape, where Doones and Ridds fight it out in pointless rivalry. Such plot as there is consists in the lovers being kept apart by events until the end of some six hundred pages. Blackmore even manages to cheat the reader of a straightforward yeoman hero and highborn heroine. A shoddier romanticism must needs see John Ridd knighted by the King and so made the equal of his Lorna. Cheating also allows the author to have Lorna apparently killed on her wedding day but later revived (almost like another Agathe from *Der Freischütz*). The book ends with a great daub of technicolour sentimental cruelty – 'I bring her to forgotten sadness, and to me for cure of it.' There they stand, huge man and tiny Lorna Doone at his shoulder, with all their money (yes, they're wealthy as well as healthy), ready to take part in any Hollywood historical film that will employ them. But such films usually have some entertainment value : even if they wished, they could never achieve the pompous tone of Blackmore's story, its Devonian clotted-cream smugness. *Lorna Doone* is a book not to drop but to throw away. There is no reason to blame it on Victorian England, where so many great or near-great novels were produced. R. D. Blackmore is the criminal and *Lorna* should now join her sisters in oblivion.

The Adventures of Huckleberry Finn

LONG before Salinger came slopping along, scuffing his foot as a sensitive adolescent, Mark Twain had crammed himself into the coy-boy uniform of patched jeans and checked shirt. Polishing his face into healthy honesty, sprinkling his features with freckles and his style with their folksy verbal equivalents, he created an all-American product. The result is canned huckleberries in the unnatural juice of homely humour, with the added colouring matter of sentimentality. Marie-Antoinette never dared to achieve anything so flagrantly false; and the myth of the countryside being 'better' has never had such an arch exponent-exploiter as Twain-Finn who ends his book by expressing his wish to light out for the Territory again: 'because Aunt Sally she's going to adopt me and sivilize me . . .' Everywhere a note of bogus nature-poetry sounds behind the wilful misspellings and whimsical grammatical mistakes (all somehow increasing the sheer lovableness, the author trusts, of his hero). This nature note is, despite American fauna and pawky humour, close to the concept of *The Wind in the Willows*: the big still river 'kind of solemn', and Huck and Jim laying [*sic*] on their backs 'looking up at the stars, and we didn't ever feel like talking loud, and it warn't often that we laughed' (well spelt, Huck, by the way). It's a man's world, where women usually just cluck on the side lines or occasionally melt away into Dickens-style unreality ('looking as sweet and contented as an angel half-full of pie').

But it is not a world of real men, only gangling boys who might be Wendy's; clean and sexless, with sort of feelings for doing the right thing by niggers, and kinda adventurous temperaments. The adolescent dream goes on, lulling the reader into an immá-ture climate where goodness somehow triumphs and yet every tribute is paid to the abstract concept of 'boyishness'.

It is a vision which can be achieved only by that ruthless dis-honesty which is the birthright of every sentimentalist. The next stage after Twain is not Salinger but Hemingway : the boy has proved father of Jake and ???????. Beyond that point it is hard to go in the sentimentality of stupidity and toughness. With these literary standards there really is no hope for sivilization.

Tess of the D'Urbervilles

PERHAPS it was Wessex clay that clogged Hardy's pen. Something certainly intervened between the sublime tragic ideas dimly
in his head and the ludicrous results when set on paper. Or
rather : nothing intervened. The spark of art refused to jump
into existence. We are left standing futilely in the soggy wet
fields of novels where the earth is the ravaged, bloodstained
scene of dreary crimes and appalling mistakes, littered with frost-
bitten decaying vegetables and plentiful corpses. It is an almost
Jacobean vision (where one might come on a severed hand while
planting potatoes), except that it never touches the nerve of true
intensity, and the pulse is more often quickened by laughter
than by horror. Among the things butchered by Hardy is unfortunately the English language. You cannot make tragedy out
of the life of Jude Fawley if you have no way to express its
central theme except by throwing gobbets of raw diction at the
reader. Jude's fundamental error was, he thought, 'that of having
based a permanent contract on a temporary feeling which had
no necessary connection with affinities that alone render a life-
comradeship tolerable'. As the plots deepen into hysterical gloom,
the stilted inadequacy of the language becomes unbearable. Time
has added an additional cruelty in making the sex in Hardy's
Wessex simply funny. Or wasn't it always fairly silly? Hardy
seems to be positively anxious to equate coition with destiny –
and his idea of destiny is not at all cheerful. This would not

much matter did he not signal his approaching threats by destiny-motifs of such ponderous cosmic gloom and elephantine tread. The simplest action picture is framed by great bulbous gilt observations until one can't see the composition for the admonitions: 'The "appetite for joy" which pervades all creation, that tremendous force which sways humanity to its purpose, as the tide sways the helpless weed, was not to be controlled by vague lucubrations over the social rubric.' That is the conclusion to Tess's acceptance of Angel Clare's proposal. When she finally marries him Hardy's band plays shrill foreboding themes of such brassy obviousness as would penetrate a deaf man's ear: the unlucky cock-crow in the afternoon, the old d'Urberville house with grim female portraits, pouring rain and an attempted suicide – all this, and the wedding night hardly begun. We are plunged into a world not of rustic reality but romantic opera, provided with a hack libretto which only the genius of Donizetti or Bellini could rise above. And underneath it all is a vein of deep cruelty, masquerading as factual, playing with the problem of a woman with a past. Angel Clare's behaviour, which Hardy is good enough to explain as rather conventional, is not only monstrous but – much worse artistic crime – unconscious. Not since medieval stories like that of patient Griselda had women been tortured as Hardy tortures Tess (and also Sue in *Jude*). Himself no president of immortals but the chairman of petty sessions, he is reluctant to let her receive the peace of death, and with sickening obtusity and deep moral conventionality, closes his book by hinting at Angel Clare's next marriage.

One final point must be made against Hardy. It is sometimes thought that his novels bring into literature a rural world that had not previously interested fiction writers. His pathetically inept Wessex is supposed to be particularly valid and true to the soil; applause greets the clumsy capers of the regional novel. But long before Hardy's lachrymose pomposities, George Eliot had created a wonderful rural world, artistically true, much more seriously ambitious in scope and much more far-ranging. Beside her achievement Hardy is the person who should be dealt with, and disposed of, not by the President of the Immortals but by us. We have finished with him.

Poems

HOPKINS'S is the poetry of a mental cripple. Sympathize as one might with his confusion, with the absurd struggle that went on within him between priest and poet, it is impossible not to end by feeling completely exasperated with the disastrous mess he made of his life. The muscle-bound, determinedly 'difficult' verse that he produced is really abhorrent. It may have a sentimental appeal to his co-religionists, but to others Hopkins is surely the most unrewarding of the Victorian poets. The interior war in his permanently bared breast between aesthetic and ascetic is a blatantly uneven combat: the aesthete scarcely exists. The man is all metaphysics, mysticism and neurotic longing for the cross. Add to these disabilities the baleful influence of Dante Gabriel and Christina Rossetti, and it is immediately apparent that poor Hopkins hadn't a chance.

In his groping attempts to find his own mode of expression, Hopkins is not unlike Browning, but he lacks completely Browning's sudden illumination. Hopkins is at the mercy both of his superstitions and of his theories. It was the theories which proved the more dangerous to his verse. His meaningless and arbitrary definitions of 'inscape' and 'instress' serve to underline the almost Nihilist emptiness of his thought. In a letter, Hopkins wrote: 'You know I once wanted to be a painter. But even if I could I would not I think, now, for the fact is that the higher and more attractive parts of the art put a strain on the passions which

I shd think it unsafe to encounter.' No wonder his poetry is so cringingly irrelevant. There is nothing brave about his obscurity: it is that of weak-mindedness and theology.

Esther Waters

GEORGE MOORE, conversing in Ebury Street into his dotage, was surely able to retain a literary reputation only because nobody bothered to read his novels. His principal, probably his only, interest was himself, so it is hardly surprising that his best work is to be found in autobiographical writings. *Memoirs of My Dead Life* and *Hail and Farewell* have an engaging warmth and humanity conspicuously absent from Moore's fiction which is, for the most part, of a fairly obvious contrivance.

It is Moore's misunderstanding of his heroes Balzac and Zola which proved his undoing as a novelist. That, and his natural inability to write a decent prose. Zola's idea of realism may have had its elements of Grand Guignol, but its dilution in the work of Moore into the equivalent of the dead and deadening Victorian problem picture results in something which falls as far short of Zola as Zola does of Balzac.

Moore himself said of *Esther Waters*: 'It is all about servants – servants devoured by betting.' And this manner of describing it shows clearly the theoretical nature of its genesis. The man who sets out with the intention of writing about betting, or even about servants, is unlikely to be a real novelist. It is not, of course, impossible for the *roman à thèse* to be a really fine *roman*, but imaginative invention is at least as necessary as the desire to produce something on servants or politics or the Industrial Revolution. Moore, in trying for the common touch, succeeded only in being commonplace. He knew a great deal about horse racing and betting, and not very much about servants. The result is a novel in which one or two big set-pieces, such as the Derby Day scenes, come off well. The greater bulk of the novel does not. For all his desire to write a work of great naturalism, Moore's prose obstinately remains an uneasy mixture of sub-mandarin and police reporter :

> The men puffed at their pipes; old John's anecdotes about the days when he and the Gaffer, in company with all the great racing men of the day, used to drive down by road, were listened to with admiration, and just as Esther finished telling Sarah the circumstances in which she had met Margaret, the train stopped outside of a little station, and the blue sky, with its light wispy clouds, became the topic of conversation, old John not liking the look of those clouds, and the women glancing at the waterproofs which they carried on their arms.

It is impossible to work up any interest in Moore's characters. Esther herself is incredibly priggish, and Mrs Barfield biliously pious. The author's own attitude to some of the events he describes has so maidenly a coyness that it is difficult to believe *Esther Waters* was published as late as 1894 when Shaw and Wilde, to name only two of the more talented of Moore's fellow-Irishmen, were enlivening the London scene. *Esther* reads like Irish stage melodrama of 1864. Repenting of having allowed herself to be seduced, Esther quite seriously remarks to Mrs Barfield : 'I shouldn't have touched the second glass of ale.' Later, advising her own sister who thinks of 'going on in the pantomime as one of the hextra ladies', Esther cries: 'Oh, Jenny, you won't do that, will you? A theatre is only sinfulness, as we 'ave always knowed.' Throughout this very long novel, the sentiments are as exemplary, the diction as unlikely. If George Moore has any usefulness as a novelist, it can only be to make Hardy appear quite readable by comparison.

A. E. HOUSMAN

Collected Poems

OF course, compared with Kipling (q.v.) or Henley or Francis Thompson (q.v.), Housman is almost bearable. But this is to apply the lowest of standards. If his verse is to be preferred to the religious bombast of Thompson, the sick, stunted Boys' Own Paper style of Henley or the war-mongering of Kipling, it is merely because he is less objectionable. Housman has few, if any, positive virtues. Actually, he too is prone to froth, ever so gently, at the mouth, at the thought of war; but, for him, the excitement appears to be brought on by the possibility of death rather than by thoughts of glory.

It doesn't matter that Housman's poetry has no intellectual content. Or, rather, it wouldn't have mattered were it not for his occasional still-born attempts at formulating a philosophy. What distresses one most is the sloppiness and imprecision of his language which is, of course, a consequence of the vague, generalized sentimentality of his feelings. And when, in an attempt to avoid sentimentality, he opts for a toughness of diction, the result is as ludicrous as the thought of Marilyn Monroe playing a rôle written for Humphrey Bogart.

The period at which he wrote can, to some extent, be blamed for the shortcomings of Housman's style. It was not easy then for a homosexual to write frankly of his feelings, and Housman had nothing in his character to equal Wilde's brave folly. Instead, he hid behind his romantic self-pity. Such an attitude was hardly conducive to the production of great poetry, and it led Housman to create nothing but thin, slovenly calendar-verse. This meagre-talented poet of adolescence, thread-bare of style, cliché-ridden in content, and as rhythmically monotonous as Brahms or Dixieland jazz, is seen at his worst in *A Shropshire Lad* which is simply one huge pathetic fallacy.

Housman's verse, bad as it is, is not even original to him. It is hardly more than the sum of a great many diverse influences such as those of Shakespeare, Kipling and the Greek poets. But, as critics have pointed out before now, there is a very strong Heine influence as well. In fact, Housman could almost be described as a Heine without sting. The characteristic bite of Heine's rhyme is lacking in Housman, but large slices of the English poet's verse are so direct an imitation of the German's as to invite a charge of plagiarism. What, for instance, is Housman's 'The living are the living/And dead the dead will stay' but an excellent translation of Heine's 'Es bleiben tot die Toten/Und nur die Lebendige lebt'? And what is the use of writing stuff like

In the morning, in the morning,
In the happy field of hay,
Oh they looked at one another
By the light of day

when Heine had done the same kind of thing half a century earlier with

Im wunderschönen Monat Mai,
Als alle Knospen sprangen,
Da ist in meinem Herzen
Die Liebe aufgegangen.

The most notorious example of Housman's indebtedness to Heine is to be found in 'Sinner's Rue':

I walked alone and thinking,
    And faint the nightwind blew
And stirred on mounds at crossways
    The flower of sinner's rue.

Where the roads part they bury
    Him that his own hand slays,
And so the weed of sorrow
    Springs at the four cross ways.

The original, one of Heine's *Lyrisches Intermezzo* poems, is much better:

Am Kreuzweg wird begraben,
Wer selber sich bracht um;
Dort wächst eine blaue Blume,
Die Armesünderblum.

Am Kreuzweg stand ich und seufzte;
Die Nacht war kalt und stumm.
Im Mondschein bewegte sich langsam
Die Armesünderblum.

The old fraud has simply switched the order of the stanzas.

The Hound of Heaven

The Spectator thought it more than held its own with Crashaw. *The Times* prophesied that it would still be learnt by heart 'two hundred years hence'. This is tepid praise compared with that offered by *The Bookman* and the Bishop of London. The latter thought it one of the most tremendous poems ever written; the former had a fit of bookish frenzy in which it screamed 'the most wonderful lyric in the language'.

Probably even the warmest admirers today of *The Hound of Heaven* would find this excessive; other people may be merely puzzled as to how the over-written rhetoric of Thompson ever imposed itself. The date of the poem's publication is a clue. It appeared in 1893, at a period when purple sins were almost as much in vogue as purple passages. After the leaden materialism of the century's middle years came the filigree refinements and exotic escapades of the nineties. Religion itself was fashionable; penitence was as promising as sin, and Swinburne had already hymned the exciting prospects of the cult of the birch goddess, Our Lady of Pain. Of religions the most fashionable was Roman Catholicism, with its drugging ritual, hints of perverse mortification, outward splendour and inner sanctity. Time had lent it a final glamour, consecrating its aspect of white-faced cardinals moving amid fans held by page boys with scarlet lips and eyes of impossible limpidity, slim fingers twisted about a jewelled rosary or a phial of poison. Wilde, Dowson, Beardsley, were all intrigued aesthetically – and finally, seriously converted. It was a period well summed up by the fact that Lionel Johnson, one more doomed Roman Catholic aesthete, wrote a Latin poem for the salvation of the soul of Richard Le Gallienne, writing it in his copy of Le Gallienne's *Religion of a Literary Man*.

To the weary, guilty hints and mystery – the passion of penitence – Thompson brought his own excited story: bursting on to the scene with a religious poem about being pursued by a *man*. Additional titillation was added not only by his flight from Him (a capital letter adding to the mystery) but by Thompson's assumption of coyness decked out with proto-Hollywood trappings. All the teasing femininity suggested by romantic films, or illustrated by advertisements for high quality soaps and shampoos is caught in the lines:

> With thy young skyey blossoms heap me over
> From this tremendous Lover!
> Float thy vague veil about me, lest He see.

It would be cruel but just to compare this with the writings of a real woman who was also a real mystic: St Theresa of Avila. There is nothing even of magnificent baroque self-delusion in Thompson's over-written work. It is maudlin with self-pity, drenched in tears that have made a large but shallow pool where language constantly collapses into false poeticisms and archaic usage – 'bruit' and 'wist', with a steady repetition of 'Lo' as if to lull us into accepting as poetry the sort of beer-mat jingle which ends up:

> Whom wilt thou find to love ignoble thee,
> Save Me, save only Me?

Because there is a happy ending, of course. The flight (conducted *à la* Swinburne, 'down the arches of the years') seems the product only of some obscure lovers' quarrel and it closes with His hand 'outstretched caressingly'. A fade-out is inevitable. The first public, dispersing somewhat baffled by the performance, was probably divided: the critics being impressed by the mysticism, while the clergy gaily turned literary and approved as 'poetry' what was bolstered by a Christian message. Both today look equally bogus. The mysticism is sheer sentimentalism, and sentimentality has sugared the language to an intolerable sweetness and complete vagueness. Many of the lines do not make sense: they merely sound as if they do. Francis Thompson was running away from himself, shouting as he went that someone was after him. If anyone *was* chasing him, it was probably the personification of English Literature – stretching out its hand to give him not a caress but a well-deserved blow.

Peter Pan

IT's not a fault – it may even lend him the virtue of a poetic elasticity – for an author not fully to comprehend his own theme. The *Oedipus Rex* is a great poetic tragedy even though Sophocles most probably never articulated the facts of the Oedipus complex to himself in so many words. Neither is any theme impermissible in itself. Incest, castration and homosexuality are proper subjects for drama – even for drama designed for children, whose own unconscious minds nightly design them fantasies on those subjects anyway. The only thing that is aesthetic murder is for an author to half-know and yet wantonly not-know – and then to tease and flirt with what he can't help, but won't admit to, knowing. Because its author plays peep-bo with his own knowledge of his theme (his theme being incest, castration and homosexuality), *Peter Pan* is an aesthetic massacre of the innocents – though it is also perhaps the most copybook example of stagecraft, of engineering an audience's emotions, in the repertory of the theatre.

The incest theme is announced at once. The children are introduced during a let's-pretend game in which John and Wendy, who are brother and sister, play-act being husband and wife and claim their brother Michael as their son. This prefigures the relation between Wendy and Peter Pan, an erotic relation, in which they flirt over a kiss and provoke Tinker Bell to sexual jealousy, but also a relation in which Wendy mothers Peter. In the Never Land, Peter introduces her to the boys as 'a mother for us all'; she is even addressed as 'mummy'; yet presently Peter is playing father.

What small boys in the throes of the Oedipus situation feel about fathers is epitomized in the casting of the same actor as Mr Darling and as the villain and danger of the piece. What small boys in that situation would like to do to fathers, the play's castration theme, is introduced with the crocodile, who has already actually snapped off one of Captain Hook's members. The animal might have been created to illustrate what Freud called 'the infantile recurrence of totemism' – and from a literary point of view there is certainly more life in the totem sea beast which pursues Barrie's sea captain than in what must surely be its model, the sea beast pursued by Melville's.

The homosexual theme Barrie does not introduce explicitly until the last act. But it has of course been present all along in the transvestite casting of Peter Pan him/herself and has been flirted at us in the play Barrie makes with that transvestism in the dialogue and action. It is an actress who, playing Peter, hurts Wendy's feelings by a display of unequivocally virile pride ('He crows like a cock') and assuages them ('the artful one', comment Barrie's stage directions) by 'popping on to the end of the bed' and assuring her 'Wendy, one girl is worth more than twenty boys'.

Girls in drag flirting with girls straight have, of course, a hundred theatrical precedents. (Barrie was denied the extra kink Shakespeare enjoyed whereby his girls were really boys, anyway.) But the history of the play's genesis in Barrie's mind contains a sex-change unique to Barrie's mind. The germ of *Peter Pan*, according to its author, was a let's-pretend game which he, already in his forties, regularly played with a family of small boys. Some tableaux from the game were made into a photograph album. A dog – or, to be exact, two successive dogs – took part in the game and appeared in the photographs. Both these real-life dogs were male. When, however, Barrie transposed the real-life dog into the dog character in the play, he changed its sex. Nana is, of course (as a nanny), female. But the rôle of the dog in the play is, of course, taken by a human. And Barrie specified that the human who played the part of the dog should be a boy.

No one who has taken in the sex-alternations of Nana can feel much surprise when, towards the end of the play, Wendy at last comes explicitly out with the homosexual theme, which she does during her account of the sex differentiation of fairies: 'the mauve fairies are boys and the white ones are girls, and there are some colours who don't know what they are'.

Barrie was almost contemporary with Freud. Both were men of genius. Both were gifted observers of children – though Barrie perhaps limited his observation to boy children. It seems unlikely he knew much about girls' fantasies, since he keeps Wendy back from an active part in the battle against the pirates; and, while he was about the free invention of a world ideal for children, he really might have seen to it that his invention freed Wendy from sewing and washing. On the other hand, it may be only by undertaking the chores that Wendy was admitted to the ideal world at all. Barrie writes of one of the earlier stages of the story as being before 'we let women in'. At her very first encounter with Peter, Wendy does a spot of mending for him. That may have been her immigration permit.

Barrie's observations, one-sided though they may be, coincided with many of Freud's. Barrie knew that the two great preoccupying questions of childhood are 'Where do babies come from?' (hence Wendy's and Peter's speculative dissertations on where fairies come from) and 'How do you tell boy babies from girl babies?' During the game where John and Wendy play-act their parental fantasy, the important question 'Boy or girl?' is rapped out four times in a minute's dialogue. *Peter Pan* is by way of being Barrie's *Interpretation of Dreams*. (Freud, four years the elder, published his four years earlier.) *Peter Pan,* subtitled 'the boy who would not grow up', is full of insights into the unconscious, that core in everyone which *cannot* grow up. Indeed, the play itself *is* a dream, as the final stage direction implies: Peter Pan 'produces his pipes' and 'plays on and on till we' (the audience) 'wake up'. Barrie's play states almost as plainly as *The Interpretation of Dreams* itself the significance of dreams of flying. (As it were: Wendy and John express their wish for a child, then fall asleep and dream of flying.) For once Barrie makes concession enough to girls' wishes to let Wendy fly, too. But of course she's shot down.

Freud, however, was an honest non-fiction thinker. Barrie was a dishonest artist. Freud saw that children have the utmost right

– who more? – to know where children come from, and that to laugh at them for their quaint ignorance of sex is a dishonourable act on the part of adults who have deliberately kept them ignorant. For taking this honourable view Freud was at first ignored and then abused as a besmircher of children's innocence. Barrie, on the other hand, became a bestseller and, presently, a baronet, largely on the strength of a play whose dialogue is one long tease of children's sexual curiosity (the last thing Barrie is prepared to do is *answer* their questions; he assures them it's much nicer for them to believe in mauve, white and indeterminately coloured fairies) and whose often very witty stage directions are one long snigger behind his adult hand at the children's quaint innocence. His most dastardly stage direction is probably the one where he actually hints that the way you get a baby is to buy it : Mr Darling, he tells us, earlier in his married life, 'did all the totting up for' Mrs Darling, 'while he calculated whether they could have Wendy or not'.

It's not enough, however, for Barrie to betray children. He betrays art. He does it brilliantly. That superb piece of engineering (the engineering, however, of an instrument of torture), the scene where Peter Pan appeals to the children in the audience to keep Tinker Bell alive by clapping to signal their belief in fairies, is a metaphor of artistic creation itself. All characters in all plays are kept alive by the audience's belief in them. But the belief properly exacted from audiences is belief of the kind Coleridge distinguished as 'poetic faith', a 'willing suspension of disbelief for the moment'. Peter Pan blackmails the children, cancels the willingness of the suspension of disbelief, and disrupts the convention on which all art depends when he threatens to hold the children morally responsible for Tinker Bell's death unless by a real act – an act done in the auditorium, not on the stage – they assert their literal belief in what they know to be an artistic fiction. It is his culminating, cleverest and most diabolical flirtation with children's innocence. By perpetrating it he destroyed his own innocence as an artist.

An Habitation Enforced

FEW writers have been so often revived as Kipling. But then few
have been so often discredited. The frequency with which critics
rediscover him – about once every five years – is a mark not of
any vitality but of his propensity for dying on his re-discoverers'
hands.

As a popular writer, Kipling still does some trade in the
children's department, not only with his children's books but also
with those he intended for adults, which have begun that slide
down the mental age scale whereby the fashionable fiction, like
the fashionable slang, of one generation fetches up, a generation
or two later, in the nursery – before it finally gets chucked into
the lumber room. Only wars can jerk Kipling back into regular
adult currency. As soon as war breaks out, out come the leather-
bound editions (Kipling seems to have run to leather more readily
than most authors), stamped with the tondo containing the elephant's head and the swastika, like pendants to the mythical
bullet-proof Bible in the soldier's breast pocket. In 1940 out
came a new anthology, *A Kipling Treasury,* of verses and short
stories 'that seemed' (to quote the blurb's sub-Churchillian – its,
indeed, Macmillanian – prose) 'specially appropriate to the times
through which we are passing'. (One further gesture appropriate
to the times was made but not mentioned by the publishers for
this edition : the binding was stamped with the tondo and the
elephant's head, but the swastika was tactfully suppressed.)

An Habitation Enforced

Re-appraisals by critics, unable in intellectual decency just to bang the patriotic drum, take the more circumspect line that Kipling's jingoism can no longer be stomached but that he should be preserved for the excellence of his technique and his mastery of, in particular, the short story form. As a matter of fact, 'jingoism' is a rather gentle name for Kipling's racialist feudalism. (The accident of his association with the swastika was not inappropriate.) All the same, it is of course true that an attack simply on his racialist feudalism would not be a literary attack. Critics have kept their eyes wide open to the dangers of extra-literary bias against Kipling (and perhaps a touch also in admiration at their own fairness) but have forgotten the danger of falling over backwards. Announcing 'Of course his jingoism is intolerable today, but . . .' they neglect to notice that his jingoism is intolerable because he didn't make it tolerable. And that is a literary failure. Kipling was not only a propagandist in a bad cause. He was a bad propagandist.

It has turned out to be Kipling's luck that he championed a cause which *no one* can nowadays stomach, with the result that he has benefited from the falling over backwards of critics of all persuasions. His technical equipment has probably received more sheer attention than any other prose writer's, and in the lime-light which was focused on it in order to avoid seeing his social and political opinions it has looked much bigger than it is. He is in fact far from a natural 'story-teller' or 'yarn-spinner'. He is inclined to edge his narratives out from his pen, often middle first, and they emerge twined with allusions, dense with phoneti-cized dialect, clotted with local colour and lame with archaic turns of phrase which have to be construed rather than read. The opening paragraph of *Kim* almost commands the reader to halt and proceed no further:

> He sat, in defiance of municipal orders, astride the gun Zam-Zammah on her brick platform opposite the old Ajaib-Gher – the Wonder House, as the natives call the Lahore Museum. Who hold Zam-Zammah, that 'fire-breathing dragon', hold the Punjab; for the great green-bronze piece is always first of the conqueror's loot.

Can it be in reflexion of Kipling's perverse tendency to thrust the wrong end of the stick at the reader that Kim has nowadays become a girl's name?

Propaganda is a technical failure if it renders its message either unreadable or, once struggled through, preposterous. It was no master of the short story form who perpetrated two of the stories selected in 1940, presumably by Kipling admirers, to rank as Kipling treasures – on the strength of (to quote the blurb again) 'their exquisite interpretation of the English countryside and its gracious influences'. *Gracious* is an odd description of the rural influences in '*They*' (Kipling's inverted commas), a story in which a narrator with an intense fixation on pre-pubescent children discovers by chance a corner of rural England where a blind woman keeps open house to the ghosts of the many pre-pubescent children who have recently died in the neighbouring village. Kipling in this *Turn of the Screw* mood only shows to advantage the artistic good sense which permeated Henry James to his very unconscious, and miraculously preserved *his* ghost story from both the mawkish and the silly.

If there is a story in English more preposterous than '*They*', it is *An Habitation Enforced,* where Kipling again takes a Jamesian turn, boasting to foreigners about rural place names (Rocketts, Pardons) which even James might have shunned (to say nothing of a minor character with the purely Jamesian name of Mrs Shonts), and tackling James's theme of frank Americans encountering reticent and complicated English. The result, however, is not James but Mrs Miniver. The supernatural is as important in this story as in '*They*', but here it assumes the less palpable shape of the myth that blood is thicker than the Atlantic Ocean. Kipling's young American millionaire couple, George and Sophie, directed to an English country house by chance, feel detained there by an attraction they do not understand. They buy the house, plus the farms on its estate, and find themselves accepted by the local gentry as equals and by the local peasantry as patricians – an acceptance not won, though he is even richer and has been trying longer, by a parvenu Brazilian, whose money was made in spices and who is described by the rustics as a 'nigger' and by Kipling, with a more refined condescension, as 'a dusky person'. George and Sophie come to understand both their mysterious compulsion towards the place and their no less mysterious acceptance in it only when they discover that Sophie is descended from a local landowner. (Would the supernatural spell not have worked had she been descended from an equally local farm labourer?) The privileges of wealth are presented as duties nobly undertaken – and boil down chiefly to the duty of tormenting the local fauna to death and compensating the local poor for their poverty by bossing their lives. ('Your people', says Lady Conant to Sophie, parcelling out the retainers between them and apologizing for 'poaching' on Sophie's parcel. Peasants, one wonders, or pheasants?) Even producing an heir to the millions and the privileges is accounted a creditable duty. ' 'Tis God's work', Sophie is comfortingly assured by a retainer who has divined her pregnancy, '. . . An' you've never failed of your duty yet.' No more does Kipling of his, when the rich, classy and of course male child is born. Kipling can't even be facetious-sentimental about him without falling into Biblical tones : 'George Lashmar wanted all the bluebells on God's earth that day to eat, and Sophie adored him in a voice like the cooing of a dove; so business was delayed.' And to be precise, the technique which Kipling's vaunted technical equipment can properly be said to have invented is that of the glossy, hollow weepie : at all the moments when such a film breaks into Bach, on the organ, with ecclesiastical echo, Kipling breaks into the cadences of the First Lesson.

Now we've got rid of the rest of the Empire, couldn't we please ditch Kipling too?

The History of Mr Polly

OF all English fictional devices, that of the put-upon, comic little man is perhaps the worst. A vulgar postcard characterization may be briefly funny, but what can be the point of setting it down at length in writing, with equal parts of condescension and sentimentality? The title of Wells' book proclaims what we are in for : there is already the implied discrepancy between a 'history' and a man with a funny name. Between Mr Polly's indigestion and his rather capriciously assigned 'hunger . . . for the gracious aspect of things, for beauty' there is the author's wobbling viewpoint which finally lands him and his little man in a great sunset dollop of sentimental happiness, sitting by a fat woman at evening on the river bank – almost like something out of *The Wind in the Willows*.

What is the point of the book? Its plot is simply that of the worm that turned. Its realism is invalidated immediately by its comico-sentimental tone, an inheritance presumably from the Dickens of *Pickwick Papers* (q.v.). Was it still possible in 1910 to utilize such whimsical antiquated conventions as the animating of the inanimate: 'The knives and forks, probably by some secret common agreement, clash and clatter together . . .'? Its comedy is on a level so puerile that it can hardly amuse anyone except its author; we are back in the funny world of Mrs Malaprop, and the humour is often a joke *against* Mr

Polly who is found saying things like: 'You've merely anti-separated me by a hair.' Other comic devices are mildly signalled by ponderous language ('Mr Polly, undeterred by a sense of grave damage to his nose . . .') and include fights which seem inspired by close study of the technique of Jerome K. Jerome. There is no distinct character to Mr Polly, because he is a piece of writer's stock material, run up clumsily in Wells' basement imagination, with hurried tacking stitches, and labelled hastily with attributes of malapropism, timidity, and – of course – fundamental decency and pluck. Wells does not even have the boldness to allow Mr Polly to run away and stay away from his wife (whose meals are the cause of his indigestion), but has him creeping back at the end. Only when it is clear that she doesn't want him to stay can Mr Polly and the reader settle to the treacly riverside finish at the Potwell Inn where Mr Polly has become a happy handyman.

Over the whole book hangs an Edwardian afterglow, suitably enough for a book published in the year Edward VII died. Little drapers, lack of education, boating, lower-class funerals; it would be easy now to touch these things with nostalgia and write a lament for flannel trousers, celluloid collars, puny men and fat, jolly ladies who keep pubs. Wells already indulged a sort of half-hearted nostalgia, uncertain whether his hero and his environment were to be admired or made fun of. Mr Polly remains finally a little man owing to the avuncular coyness of his creator who in his busy active career committed almost every artistic sin. Wells mistakenly detected an aridity and pretentiousness in Henry James, priding himself on having common sympathies and a common touch. But for all his boasting, it was he who had the tone of insufferable condescension, expressed by a style which constantly sought the genteel periphrases of literary journalism. With his leaden facetiousness went a patronage of human beings much more distasteful than any mandarin remoteness could possibly be. Wells picks up his homunculus Polly, a worm caught on the unsubtle pitchfork of his stylistic affectation, and has his superior fun: 'I have hinted that our Mother England had equipped Mr Polly for the management of his internal concerns no whit better than she had for the direction of his external affairs.'

And Mother England had not equipped H. G. Wells any better for the management of anything to do with literature. *The History of Mr Polly* may be Wells' revenge for having had to serve an apprenticeship in a draper's shop, but the motive proved not sufficiently powerful to produce a valid work of art.

JOHN GALSWORTHY

The Forsyte Saga

UNTIL recently there was no danger of this book getting into anyone's list of serious English masterpieces, and little reason therefore to shoot down its pretensions. However, the conspiracy of
newspapers and TV to try to fascinate us with either Galsworthy's
own life story or his story of the Forsytes is probably already
affecting people. Soon it will be asked, how can it not be a
masterpiece? And to some extent it might be urged that in the
category of good-bad book Galsworthy's is a masterpiece. Within
his own oeuvre, incidentally, it is not necessarily his best piece of
writing. Those intent on making him out a great writer would
be well advised to pay some attention to *The Country House* –
a less deeply romantic work – that is, a less self-indulgent one.

The Forsyte Saga betrays its rickety status as a classic by what
can be described only as its inner poverty. The closer Galsworthy comes to the vital principle of people, the more frankly
melodramatic and shoddy does his language become. He is deft
at observing the old aunts in the house on the Bayswater Road –
deft without being particularly profound. When he has to deal
with the presumed passionate nature of Irene he stoops to quite
meaningless clichés, babbling about 'the eternal verities' in terms
which suggest Lady Elinor Glyn. She in fact might have handled
more convincingly the love affair between Irene and the shadowy
architect, Bosinney. The Saga's two themes, meant to be subtly
entwined, are sexual passion and property. Galsworthy is deeply

respectful of the first, but writes as if he had never experienced it; about the second he is ironic, mistrustful, anxious to make it account for nameless evils, and yet is instinctively able to respond to its appeal. The memorable characters in the book are the oldest generation – the ones, that is, seen most from the outside, the most heavily 'made-up', with wrinkles, whiskers and period costumes – who give the book such resonance as it has. By making frequent use of two dangerously slick literary devices -- ageing and death – Galsworthy achieves effects of pathos which are both true to life and artistically trite. They are victories won by appealing to the shallowest emotions, the tears of a spinster at a stranger's wedding. The death of old Jolyon – which even manages to include his dog in a manner recalling the worst excesses of Landseer – is one of such moments: the author seems to defy us not to be moved by the fact of death, even while wrapping this in sloppy pseudo-lyrical prose which is sentimental and false. The same pat effect is attempted by the long family chronicle narration which seeks but fails to suggest an emotional perspective behind the love affairs of a young generation who do not know what the reader knows.

This young generation is perhaps the most obvious sign of Galsworthy's basic triteness. As he approaches his own contemporary world of the 1920s, his characters become quite patently thin, increasingly seen in stock situations and responding with second-hand emotions. The artifice of the whole book is abruptly clear: a conventional flapper-ish girl – Fleur – stands for her generation, with behind her the wistful property-obsessed generation represented by her father, Soames. And behind him is the full Victorian solidity of his father, James. Mouthpieces of their generations, they are not truly characters but personifications in Galsworthy's version of *Cavalcade*. The whole thing is an extended charade: a caricature of real theatre, as it is a caricature of real people and emotions. There are dangerous enough moments in *War and Peace,* a book which, significantly, Galsworthy thought the greatest novel ever written. Consciously or not, he was aiming at an English replica of that. What he produced was a pseudo-classic: a thoroughly middle-class substitute for real literature. Despite its length, the Forsyte Saga is really no more than a novelette.

South Wind

THE heat haze clears about the outline of this book and its real insignificance becomes increasingly apparent as more and more people go to Italy for its own sake – not merely to meet their fellow-countrymen – and fewer and fewer people mistake pseudo-learning for literature. A good book is not automatically written by composing a Platonic dialogue of un-Platonic length, spicing it with pastiche history and would-be witty hagiography, and assembling a cast of sub-intellectual speakers. The plot of *South Wind* is as non-existent as its atmosphere. Its Italy is a richly coloured romantic pagan land that might have been dreamt up in Wimbledon in 1917 – but hardly by someone who had actually lived in Italy. Douglas produced an unpalatable sandwich of invented facts and semi-true fictions: alternate layers of the indigestibly hard and the displeasingly mushy. Priding himself on being incisive and sub-acid about the local saint, cult or legend, he took a brush dripping with water colour to wash-in the character of Denis and the long-winded self-exposés of Mr Keith.

There is probably still a feeling among the semi-educated that *South Wind* is a *literary* book, somehow superior as literature – of the type beloved by critics – to a merely creative novel in which the people are not intellectuals. The one undoubted fact about *South Wind* is the dreadfully fecund effect it had, planting tiny seeds of mistaken confidence in the minds of several uncreative writers and generating a number of imitations. A collection of comic English characters abroad became a stock opening situation, offering all the opportunities already grabbed by Douglas to show off knowledge (preferably by inventing some local saint or painter) and to make conversation consist of tepid party-going intellectual exchanges. Above all, it offered the opportunity to coast along with a reputation as a novelist while never actually writing a proper novel. The real begetter by accident of that sort of writer was naturally no novelist himself; it was Landor. However, among his advantages was brevity, as well as a marvellously forged prose style. The shoddy manner of Douglas when he was not showing off – the journeyman style needed to stretch *South Wind* to over four hundred pages – anticipates the drudging prose of Aldous Huxley, the same tired lapse towards the nearest available cliché, like an exhausted old clubman into a leather armchair: 'When the bibliographer's eagle eye first fell upon this passage he was staggered.'

But if *South Wind* has no style, no plot, no real characters, no value as truth and less as an authentic fictional structure – what has it got? It has the reputation of its author as a wit to sustain it. His reputation as a wit rests on the book. And we need no Euclid to define that as a vicious circle.

W. SOMERSET MAUGHAM

The Moon and Sixpence

EVEN those critics who describe the later novels of Maugham as cynical pot-boiling are likely to be reverent about such early works as *Liza of Lambeth, Of Human Bondage* and *The Moon and Sixpence*. It is suggested by some of them that *Of Human Bondage* is Maugham's one great novel, but it appears that *The Moon and Sixpence*, which has also had a great deal of critical acclaim as a minor masterpiece of twentieth-century fiction, is the more popular.

It must be admitted that there are worse popular novelists than Maugham. He himself once proclaimed that he considered his chief function as a novelist was to entertain. The remark has a certain air of defiance; but, in a sense, the first (if not necessarily the prime) function of a novelist, of *any* artist, is to entertain. If the poem, painting, play or novel does not immediately engage one's surface interest then it has failed. Whatever else it may or may not be, art is also entertainment. Bad art fails to entertain. Good art does something in addition. Maugham's limitation as an artist is that he is equipped to do no more than entertain, and that in consequence he achieves no more than his immediate aim. He is working always at the frontiers of his meagre imagination, and the talents that he undoubtedly possesses are not, in themselves, sufficient to sustain one's interest in his narrative.

Part of the trouble is that Maugham places far too heavy an emphasis on narrative. He was always at great pains to describe himself as a story-teller; but stories as such lack resonance. Any idiot can tell a story : only an artist of imagination can tell it significantly. Maugham lacks intellectual imagination. At his best he was a good reporter – a slightly superior Galsworthy.

The Moon and Sixpence is not even good Maugham, because he forsook the straight line of narrative which he had proved he could handle quite capably, and attempted to produce something more pretentious, essayish in manner, literary in tone. He was probably driven to change his methods by the simple fact that the story of the ostensible protagonist, Charles Strickland, has not in itself sufficient solidity for a full-length novel. Hence the pseudo-autobiographical digressions, and the inordinate amount of attention given to those shoddily cardboard characters, Dick and Blanche Stroeve. Maugham once strongly advised aspiring novelists to 'stick to the point'. It is sound advice, and one wishes he had followed it himself in *The Moon and Sixpence*. As it is, the thin narrative line is decked out with a great deal of material that has the air of not belonging in the novel at all.

The character of Strickland was said by Maugham to be based on Gauguin. Certainly the bare facts of the story follow those of Gauguin's own life, and it is true that Maugham on his visit to Tahiti talked to many people who had known Gauguin, and used some of them in the novel. Lovina Chapman becomes Tiaré Johnson. Dr Paul Vernié who treated Gauguin during his last illness becomes Dr Coutras. But even the fact that one knows these people are real does not help one to believe in them in *The Moon and Sixpence*. Maugham can observe, but he cannot create. His Strickland bears not the slightest resemblance to Gauguin, or to any artist. One gets from reading this book, not the portrait of a genius but merely a string of theatrically cynical reflections on life and human behaviour, tacked on to an unconvincing story. One's objection is not that the writer really knew and could depict no one but himself, but that it is so superficial and transparent a self. His capacity to feel is smothered under blankets of cynicism and sentimentality.

The novel purports to be a reminiscence of Strickland told by someone who knew him. Unfortunately its first-person narrator seems much more concerned with himself than with the genius he is writing about. The characters, whatever names the author may have chosen to give them, are the same extensions of his own personality who litter the pages of his other novels. Maugham's conception of the amoral artist is as vulgar as Puccini's in *La Bohème*. Worse, it is more listlessly executed. And the remote sub-*belles-lettres* style that Maugham affects is not exactly lively to read. Nor has the writer whom St John Ervine (there's a name to conjure with) called a better dramatist than Congreve got much of an ear for dialogue. He has a window dresser's idea of elegance, and a shop assistant's concept of romance. When he writes of Tahiti his language is that of a travel agent.

The best that can be said of *The Moon and Sixpence* and, for that matter, of Maugham's entire oeuvre, is that it is admirable middle-brow stuff, ideally geared to the demands of the stockbroker who likes to parade his literacy but has no taste for literature.

And the best that can be said of Maugham is that at least, as far as one can see, he professed no moral standards.

To the Lighthouse

No, no, is one's reaction to the title. And, indeed, to the whole book. All that quivering, shivering, semi-luminous fabric which is not life but serves to drape in artistic folds over life. Virginia Woolf's work is like some beautifully painted, delicately tinted old parchment which has been made into a lampshade after a labour of several years. It has been done very carefully, with a great deal of thoughtful application, and with taste. Life is rather like that, Lily thought . . . Actually, Lily doesn't think quite that thought, but she is given a stream of consciousness equally banal. She shares this with the other characters in the book; despite their different names and sexes, they all fuse into being one character – not Mrs Ramsay but Mrs Woolf.

Mrs Woolf holds in her hands – or rather rocks gently on her lap but with hands lightly extended over it as if guarding its fragility – this exquisitely wrought parchment lampshade. She is wondering what to do with it. Her thoughts will in a moment go flying off, not probably at anything so sharply direct as a tangent but in some graceful parabola which trails behind it a row of dots. The lampshade will turn into an exotic flower, perhaps a water-lily of ivory pallor which will float against the sea-green material of her tweed skirt. The skirt itself, with its surprisingly rough texture, may prompt another of what she calls 'thoughts' : recalling the sensation of going up the cottage stairs, brushing against the wall as one inevitably had to in the confined space, of that absurd little place they had lived in before Prue was born ... But that's over and done with. Back she comes to reality. She looks again at the lampshade and gives it several severe stitches round the edge, just to keep it from unwinding. Nonsense really, all this dreaming. How one deplores it! It wastes time. Yet there remains something flower-like about a lampshade, let the men say what they will. She wonders why they don't come and get their coffee; yes, just as she thought, it has gone cold and the maid will have to make fresh. Each coffee cup is like a miniature, inverted lampshade. The lampshade, as she abruptly stops rocking it, is rather like life. But is that really true?

What *is* true is that many pages can be filled on this principle. What is not true is that the result can be called a novel. It is often supposed that Virginia Woolf brought to the novel a particular quality called 'art'. Her novels would by this definition not be naturalistic: a trip to the lighthouse would have a symbolic importance; events would take second place compared with sensations and thoughts; the 'pattern' of life would dominate mysteriously; people would themselves be treated as works of art. All this 'art' is indeed in Virginia Woolf's books. Before she settles down to make her lampshade, she lays out the materials for our admiration. In one delicate hand she lifts up the delicate skein of ribbon which she intends to bind it with: we exclaim at the subtle colour, immediately seeing how effective it will look woven in and out. So much artistry must announce a work of art. And yet the result remains very much a lampshade. And far from being remote from life, as we were expecting, far from being over-intellectual, it is positively homely. Virginia Woolf has filled the novel with people as banal as (if not, indeed, much more banal than) ourselves. They may look like precious works of art, and skill may have gone into evoking their mental processes; but the unremitting triviality of their minds is comparable to nothing human, being closest perhaps to the dripping of a faulty tap. They constantly exclaim about being alive – perhaps nagged by some doubt on the subject. For the rest, they have the past to think about, their painting or their knitting, their visual senses to keep keen (but seldom their aural ones) and Life. Quite what this is none of them know, but they suspect it's important. 'There it was before her – life. Life: she thought but she did not finish her thought.' This is not parody. It might come from any of the novels (probably does) but may be read in *To the Lighthouse* which is usually considered one of Virginia Woolf's finest achievements.

But what is the artistic achievement of reducing human experience to the gossipy level of the shallowest layer of consciousness? We are all conducting Virginia Woolf novels inside ourselves all day long, thinking how the sunset clouds look like crumbling cheese, wondering why the dinner party guests don't go, puzzling about children growing up, noticing for the first time the colour of a bus ticket. This famed sensitivity is everybody's birthright; and probably Virginia Woolf was applauded first by those who were delighted to find literary expression of their own commonplace sensations. To have those put in a book and called a novel . . . Only dots can do justice to their delight. To compare the results with James or Proust would occur only to the Eng. Lit. mind, always timid before the vigour of real art and always happiest with genteel diluted versions of it. Virginia Woolf's is a supreme example of the non-art that is at the same time inevitably (for the art v. life dichotomy is a false one) devoid of vitality. Those who praise Mrs Woolf's work should be honest with themselves. They are a potential audience for today's equivalent : Mrs Dale's Diary.

D. H. LAWRENCE

Lady Chatterley's Lover

BRITISH thought and actions about books are bedevilled by five
cumulative, though mutually contradictory, absurdities: (i) To
consider a novel obscene, and therefore in need of suppression,
because it's about sexual intercourse. (Suppose it *did* incite its
readers to copy it? Sexual intercourse is not illegal. Murder and
robbery are. But novels about those are not thought obscene and
are not suppressed.) (ii) To consider that four-letter words signi-
fying sexual intercourse are in need of suppression. (If the act
isn't, how can its name be?) (iii) To consider that, if a book *were*
a public danger, the danger would be lessened (instead of aggra-
vated) by 'literary merit'. (iv) To ban *Fanny Hill*, which doesn't
contain four-letter words, and exempt *Lady C.*, which does. (v)
To find that the charming, shapely and prettily written *Fanny
Hill* doesn't contain enough 'literary merit' to purchase exemp-
tion, whereas *Lady C.* does.

In fact, whatever merit *Lady C.* may have, it isn't literary.
The book is a straightforward novelette, which fabricates a wish-
fulfilment love affair between a very commonplace novelettish
hero, who is silent ('In his silence he seemed lost to her') and
manly in the old-fashioned conventional sense ('He hated mouth
kisses'), though given to whimsy ('John Thomas', etc.), and who
has hitherto romantically believed himself finished with the
delights of love ('suddenly he was aware of the old flame . . .
that he had hoped was quiescent for ever'), and an equally

133

commonplace titled novelettish heroine who has given up hope of ever experiencing them – until the hero's proletarianness (denoted by dialect phoneticized à la Kipling: what *can* be the point of making Mellors pronounce it 'thurty'? Don't we all?) enthralls her in a purely Eleanor-Glyn-like spell: 'her will had left her. A strange weight was on her limbs.' It is in the pure tone of pulp, down to the exclamation marks, that Lawrence gasps out Lady C.'s sensations: 'And now in her heart the queer wonder of him was awakened. A man! The strange potency of manhood upon her!'

Indeed, all that removes *Lady C.* from the run of under-the-hair-drier reading is, so far as content goes, the philistinism with which it ridicules Sir Clifford for liking Racine, and, so far as style goes, the words which Lawrence, with the noble if humourless intention of restoring meaning to what had degenerated into expletives, took down from the public lavatory wall. He seems to have picked up at the same time a sprinkling of public lavatory officialese: after his first sexual act with Lady C., Mellors 'stood a few moments, apparently adjusting his own clothing'.

1914 Sonnets

IT may seem hardly fair to set up the sad figure of Rupert Brooke simply in order to knock it down again; but to far too many people he is still *the* poet of the First World War. The man who has never even heard of Wilfred Owen, let alone read his sharply ironic poems of war, will yet be able to quote by heart a large slice of 'If I should die, think only this of me'.

The same man is probably vaguely aware that, having written that blush-making sonnet, Brooke had the grace to be killed in the war (to die of septicaemia on a French ship in the Aegean, in fact), but he most likely imagines that the lad was barely eighteen years old. As it happens he was twenty-eight and ought to have outgrown that kind of romantic poppycock a good ten years earlier. Can it be that the war which so sharpened Owen's sensibilities blunted Rupert Brooke's? To be still playing about with nostalgically self-pitiful fantasies during the war, and in one's late twenties, can hardly be considered to augur a great future as a poet.

Brooke was a nice, clean, public-school boy with a proper admiration for the worst efforts of Rossetti and Swinburne. What more natural than that he should try his hand at writing verse? He must have been an agreeable and engaging adolescent: embarrassingly, he was still playing the same rôle almost a decade later.

As a War Poet Brooke hardly begins to exist. The authoritative new voice from the trenches that one hears is that of Wilfred Owen. Here was a newly awakened intelligence, a real compassion, and a rich and varied poetic talent working at the frontiers of language and feeling. By comparison, Brooke's poetical effusions were inept and outmoded. His unformed style leant heavily on the traditional, and for subject-matter he chose the accepted trappings of polite Georgian verse. His early peace-time poems, apart from sounding astonishingly middle-aged for so young a writer, have almost no identifying quality at all. The five *1914 Sonnets* on which his fame largely rests are frankly awful. The first one begins 'Now, God be thanked Who has matched us with His hour'. The twenty-seven year old man reacts like a pubescent child at the glorious possibilities of going off to fight a jolly war 'as swimmers into cleanness leaping'. He plunges into this healthy cold-shower war having, apparently, been involved with 'half-men, and their dirty songs and dreary. And all the little emptiness of love', which sounds as though Henry James had been singing to him, and worse, perhaps in a Turkish bath. At any rate, the poet has 'known shame' and can't wait to redeem himself in manly combat.

In the second sonnet he tells us how safe a thing is war. 'And if those poor limbs die, safest of all'. Safe from the advances of Henry James, perhaps? ('Rupert Brooke, young, happy, radiant, extraordinarily endowed and irresistibly attaching' James wrote of him a year after Brooke's death.)

In the third sonnet the bugler blows out 'over the rich Dead!' The sickening final quatrain must be quoted in full:

Honour has come back as a king, to earth,
And paid his subjects with a royal wage.
And nobleness walks in our ways again;
And we have come into our heritage.

Brooke's romantic death-wish continues through *Sonnet IV*. Number V is the best known, and the poet's 'richer dust' is enhancing the value of 'some corner of a foreign field'.

But enough. The moral is plain: Don't go in for flag-waving if you're limp-wristed.

Collected Poems

THE ups and downs of Edith Sitwell's literary reputation have been more than adequately charted over the years. There have, in fact, been rather more downs than ups. The quite witty *Façade* poems of the twenties, Poulenc-like and indeed set to Poulenc-like music by the young iconoclast William Walton, were widely acclaimed. They have been solemnly overpraised at times, but no matter. What does matter is that it has now become intellectually respectable to claim that during the war years of the forties, the poetess cast off the flippancies of her earlier manner, and assumed the mantle of greatness. If Edith Sitwell's posthumous reputation is still reasonably high in the charts, it is mainly because of those war-time poems. A glance, however, at the poems themselves should be sufficient to convince any person reasonably sensitive to words and to language that it is the early Sitwell who has the real, if seriously limited, talent. By attempting in later years to inflate her gift, she succeeded merely in dispersing it.

Old
  Sir
    Faulk
Tall as a stork,
Before the honeyed fruits of dawn were ripe, would walk,
And stalk with a gun

The reynard-coloured sun,
Among the pheasant-feathered corn the unicorn has torn,
   forlorn the
Smock-faced sheep
Sit
  And
    Sleep;

This, from *Façade*, is agreeably unpretentious and even quite
euphonius. By the nineteen-forties, however, high seriousness has
swallowed up Edith Sitwell's gift for light verse. She has become
a seer, a prophetess whose oracular utterances drop with grim
heaviness upon the page. Reviewers of the time maintained that
the ironic comedy of her earlier manner had given way to deep
feeling. But, as Mallarmé once pointed out, poetry is made of
words, not feelings. And Edith Sitwell's extravagant, rhetorical
words were, in any case, less indicative of feeling than of pomposity. Her verse of the forties abounds in Fire and Sun and
Earth and Death. The initial caps proliferate.

We did not heed the Cloud in the Heavens shaped like the
  hand
Of man . . . But there came a roar as if the Sun and Earth
  had come together –

A sudden thought : can she have been trying to write verse in
the style of Churchill's war speeches? Whatever her intention,
this is the language not of feeling but of someone who has
nothing to communicate and who seeks to conceal the fact
behind a barrage of manner. The diction is archaic, the sym-
bolism inept. How, one wonders, could this poet sustain a serious
reputation? The answer may be that Edith Sitwell acted the
rôle of great poetess to perfection. Her long velvet gown, chunky
jewellery, Plantagenet hat and Delphic quasi-smile had a hyp-
notic effect on the audiences to whom she read her poems.
Admittedly, after the first two or three, one's attention was likely
to wander away from the 'amber blood in porphyry veins'. It
was not necessary to listen closely to language of such cushioned
over-elaboration : half heard, it sounded more convincing.

Notes on 'The Waste Land'

It is folly to expect a songbird to utter truths about the universe. The folly becomes ludicrous when the songbird himself claims to do so: and shameful when people believe his claim.

Coleridge, precisely because he possessed an intellect as well as a gift, was sensible enough not to read profundities into the beautiful opium-image of *Xanadu* and wisely left it to J. L. Lowes to elucidate even his train of associations. The fuss and scandal about Swinburne died out as soon as it was realized that his long, loping, memorable lines were simply bounding with the high spirits of a goat and had no intellectual content whatever. Swinburne was the village feeble-mind who happened to possess the gift of unmeditated verbal melody. His verses remain excellent matter for declaiming hypnotically aloud on lazily crazy undergraduate summer afternoons. The same, as Anthony Blanche in *Brideshead Revisited* discovered, is true of T. S. Eliot.

By the time Eliot was making fine meshes of sound by interlacing his own imagery with quotations from Dante and Ezekiel, the 'modern movement' had liberated poetry and painting from the obligation to have subject matter and intellectual meaning. Unfortunately Eliot declined to use that freedom. As early as 1922 he was insisting on decking out *The Waste Land* with a set of prosy notes. The nice onomatopoetic effect of

> To where Saint Mary Woolnoth kept the hours
> With a dead sound on the final stroke of nine

was saddled with the flat exegesis 'A phenomenon which I have often noticed'. By 1949 the notes had, so to speak, got into the text. Lines every bit as flat as 'A phenomenon which I have often noticed' masquerade, in *The Cocktail Party,* as lines of verse. Eliot, no longer satisfied with the amusingly enigmatic effect of 'Fragments of an Aristophanic Melodrama', had insisted on filling in the gaps and putting a complete melodrama on the stage. The characters were made to use the bitten-off diction of Noël Coward, but with the wit bitten-off too. One of these banal lines might be passing judgment on them all:

> I don't know, I'm sure. They could hardly be worse.

Eliot attempted to endow the story he was so flatly telling with religious significance, his method being to borrow the corny symbolic device of the unidentified guest which had been used to similar purpose in Jerome K. Jerome's *The Passing of the Third Floor Back.* Audiences puzzled over *The Cocktail Party* much as Victorian gallery-goers puzzled over the year's 'problem picture' at the Royal Academy. Eliot's audiences ought, however, to have been prepared for the simple solution to the seeming problem (Answer: There is no answer), since his *Four Quartets* had already provided the clue by opening with a lapidary sequence, in which the staccato syllables fell in austere isolation and portentous rhythm but proved, if one was not too awed to examine them, to be explaining only that time consists of past, present and future.

> The nightingales are singing near
> The Convent of the Sacred Heart
> But one of them insists we hear
> Him undertake a heavier part
>
> In which his bird-brain will give out   5
> Profound banalities about
> The relation in which the tenses stand,
> The Anglican communion and
> Tradition's rôle in modern art.
>
> *The Waste Land* with glide and trill   10
> Issues from his songbird's bill
> While his hinder end lets drop
> Waste matter: plop plop plop.

Enter CHORUS of twentieth century Elders (Teilhard de Chardin, C. G. Jung and T. S. Eliot)

CHORUS (in unison)

We are the hollow grand old men.

*

Notes

Line 9. It is possible to read, for 'tradition', 'quotation'.

Line 13. These droppings are not 'liquid' (vide *Sweeney Among the Nightingales,* line 39), but very solid.

General Note. It may be that the means whereby T. S. Eliot prevailed upon the world to mistake him for a major poet was the simple but efficient confidence trick of deliberately entitling one or two of his verses, as though thereby to differentiate them from the rest, 'Minor Poems'.

Point Counter Point

ONE of the least known – and least bad – of Aldous Huxley's books is a critical essay called *Vulgarity in Literature,* a title which might be describing the rest of Huxley's oeuvre.

In the twenties and thirties Huxley wrote like a vulgar cynic and in the forties and fifties like a vulgar witch doctor – an effect that is probably unjust to an honest and sometimes acute mind which was, however, simply not the mind of a writer. Huxley suffered from the totally disabling defect that he didn't like words. True, words poured from him : not only many books but long books. It takes him more than four hundred pages to make his point counter point. But he expelled words as if they were noxious matter he wanted to be quickly voided of – waste matter, which he quite literally wasted by letting them accumulate in uneconomic and un-telling heaps. 'She might have reminded him', says paragraph three of *Point Counter Point*'s opening chapter, 'of the time when he never went out in the evenings without her. She might have done so; but she wouldn't; it was against her principles; she didn't want to force his love in any way.' The information, scarcely terse in the writing or subtle and original in the psychology to begin with, is given all over again in paragraph five : 'she knew that her importunity would only annoy him, only make him love her the less. But . . . the words broke out in spite of her principles.'

The impression of vulgarity was probably produced by

Huxley's distaste for the material which literature inevitably consists of. He writes in the half clinical, half with-genteel-attention-averted manner of someone obliged to clean the lavatory. He treats as noisome not only his own words but most of the foreign words and the quotations he has swallowed. These, too, he hastens to expel haphazard over his pages – hence the effect of show-off erudition, as though he were writing 'The Superficial Sixth-Former's Guide to World Culture Including God and Sex'.

Disliking the material of literature, he naturally doesn't dabble in it long or hard enough to shape his distress epigrammatically; it comes out as a mere vague sneer. But he does sometimes employ words (usually ready-made phrases in the form of scientific names) with precision – for the purpose of dirtying a tempting image: witness, for example, the account in *Antic Hay* of Gumbril's love for 'a boy of his own age', who, the next term, 'had "come out" – *Staphylococcus pyogenes* is a lover of growing adolescence – with spots and boils all over his face and neck. Gumbril's affection ceased as suddenly as it had begun.'

Huxley's technique was too slapdash for drawing characters (even his caricatures from the famous and/or literary life are scarcely recognizable); and in his eagerness to get through with what seemed to him a nasty business he did not stay to shape forms or even plots that were more than quite cleverly improvised pot-boilings. (The utmost one can admire is his cheek.) He was a novelist of intellectual ideas, a Peacock – but quite without Peacock's superb dandyism. Huxley was prepared to clothe his improvisations in any old coy figleaf or second-hand Edwardian facetiousness: after relating a conversation in a car about vulgarity (a subject which seems to have held a lethal allure for him), he lets his own narrative in *Point Counter Point* fall into the soiled vulgarity of 'An obstructing street island compelled him to fall back, but not before the taxi-driver had had time to throw doubts on his legitimacy, his heterosexuality, and his prospects of happiness in another world'. Small wonder that the cynic who treated words with such contemptuous clumsiness ended as a mystic extolling experiences which go beyond the power of words to express. Or was it that *he* lacked the power to use them expressively?

On the title page of his copy of *Point Counter Point* Scott Fitzgerald wisely wrote 'A very poor novel, what I've read of it'.

WILLIAM FAULKNER

The Sound and the Fury

It need surprise no one that in the thirties and forties Faulkner was profitably employed by Hollywood as a script-writer on films made from other authors' novels. He is, after all, a prototype of the Hollywood writer, churning out the kind of story ostensibly so advanced in its subject matter as to be shocking to the bourgeoisie, but really pandering to conventional and even retrogressive ideas of morality and religion. Addicted to alcohol like Scott Fitzgerald and to, in his later works, a convoluted prose style like Patrick White, he has neither the naive genius of the one nor the intellectual toughness of the other. That Faulkner was attracted by themes of violence is, of course, no criticism of him. That his attitude to his own writing developed over the years from cynicism into pomposity is, similarly, no guarantee of mediocrity. But when one examines the novels themselves, one realizes the irrelevance of the interminable critical discussions of Faulkner's enigmatic personality. Whether the man was a simple, kind farmer or a brutally vicious crypto-Fascist, the writer was nothing more than a vain and humourless purveyor of turgid Southern tosh. A Tennessee Williams minus the poetry, a pseudo-intellectualized Erskine Caldwell. On the occasion of his being awarded the Nobel Prize he made an incredible speech in which the vanity of the Grand Old Man (as when he referred to his own writings as 'a life's work in the agony and sweat of the human spirit, not for glory, and least of all for profit, but to create out of the materials of the human spirit something which did not exist before') trumpets forth in juxtaposition with the hick revivalist that lurks under the skin of many an apparently respectable American writer (as when he recommended 'the old veritable truths of the heart, the old universal truths lacking which any story is ephemeral and doomed – love, honour and pride and compassion and sacrifice'). There is inflated talk, too, of indomitable man enduring and prevailing. 'And ever at my side I hear/The background music swelling near', he might well have confessed.

We could easily do without the entire oeuvre of William Faulkner. The unrewarding and arbitrary difficulty of his later manner, the pot-boiling shoddiness of his earlier, the pretentious tarting-up of the simple into the significant, the clumsy listlessness of long stretches of his prose at every stage of his career, the slipshod thinking, the conventional melodrama of his bleary view of the world, his stultifying self-consciousness, all combine to brand him as essentially second-rate. If one novel must be singled out for dismissal, let it be *The Sound and the Fury*, a useful compendium of Faulkner's vices.

The Silver Chair

You can't fake a myth. No amount of donnishly going through the sagas and cycles, noting the runic and riddling speech mannerisms here and the prevalence of Witch-Queen figures there will avail : if your language and your imagination are flat, your repetitive riddling instructions (' "I will tell you, child", said the Lion. "These are the signs by which I will guide you in your quest. First; as soon as . . . But the first step is to remember. Repeat to me, in order, the four signs" ') will read merely like the instructions on a frozen food packet, and your Witch-Queen ('the Lady of the Green Kirtle, the Queen of Underland. She stood dead still in the doorway, and they could see her eyes moving as she took in the whole situation') will no more than similar personages concocted by Walt Disney transcend the *femme fatale* of a suburban tennis club. You cannot fake the ambiguous morality of myths by simply whispering your own prejudices behind your hand ('It was "Co-Educational", a school for both boys and girls, what used to be called a "mixed" school; some said it was not nearly so mixed as the minds of the people who ran it. These people had the idea that boys and girls should be allowed to do what they liked . . . All sorts of things, horrid things, went on which at an ordinary school would have been found out and stopped in half a term . . . the people who did them were not expelled or punished'). You will not buy your child readers' confidence, if you are writing, as C. S. Lewis was, in 1953, by making your narrative address them with a facetiousness and in a slang their fathers would have found old-fashioned ('His name unfortunately was Eustace Scrubb, but he wasn't a bad sort'). And when you attempt a linguistic high-flight for a noble and magical character, you should avoid mixing the vocabulary and cadences of chivalry with those of the boardroom: 'It would not have suited well either with my heart or with my honour', declares the prince at the climactic moment of the plot, 'to have slain a woman' – having begun his previous sentence with 'Yet I am glad, gentlemen'.

Neither, of course, can you fake a classic. Lewis's 'seven Chronicles of Narnia, which were published annually from 1950 to 1956, have already taken their place among the great children's classics', the note 'About the Author' at the back of the paperback edition authoritatively informs the children. If so, the sooner they're displaced the better. Back to Underland with them. (And up, as a children's classic, with T. H. White.)

A Farewell to Arms

'It is so flattering,' said Gertrude Stein of Hemingway, 'to have a pupil who does it without understanding it.' And indeed there is no quicker route to appreciating Gertrude Stein's small but true talent than to contemplate the coarse, crass mess Hemingway made when he simply slapped her *faux-naïf* style on to his own larger canvases without in the least understanding the peculiarity and sensibility of her vision.

Gertrude Stein was literate and articulate enough· to be a great picker of words. (When she found the right one, she repeated it precisely *because* it was the right one.) She was, as she claimed, a fine – and also a versatile – shaper of sentences. Her descents into bathos are calculated: they leave her standing inelegantly but foursquarely there, like Queen Victoria not being amused.

What in Gertrude Stein is disdain of affectation becomes in Hemingway the coyest affectation of all, an aping of the tongue-tied college boy who will not permit his vocabulary to stretch beyond 'lovely' in case the other chaps think him soft. 'It was lovely in the nights' is Hemingway's reticent account of the love affair in *A Farewell To Arms*. In place of Gertrude Stein's varied, and purposefully varied, cadences, Hemingway ties one short, blunt instrument to another by means of *and*: 'She had a lovely face and body and lovely smooth skin too. We would be lying together and I would touch her cheeks and her forehead and under her eyes and her chin and throat with the·tips of my fingers and say . . .' (This is from a paragraph of three sentences containing fourteen *ands*. The repetition of *lovely* in that first sentence is presumably done on the opposite of the Gertrude Stein principle – that is to say, having hit on the wrong word, Hemingway repeats it because he *still* can't think of the right one.) Gertrude Stein, like Bernard Shaw, ignores the conventional rules of punctuation both consistently and with the licence earned by knowing them; Hemingway dashes down what he takes to be the Italian for 'sister' and misspells it (' "Sorrela?" I asked'), splashes over his pages the half-literate vocabulary of a Victorian provincial sporting journalist ('commenced to eat'), makes his characters deliver sentences which start colloquially and end with an improbably literary turn (' "They got right up in the car the minute I motioned to them" ') and can tie his own narrative into knots that negate not only grammar but sense, so that he implies that the impersonal 'it' which rains can also come home and that a thing can be simultaneously indoors and outside: 'Coming home from the Ospedale Maggiore it rained very hard and I was wet when I came in. Up in my room the rain was coming down heavily outside on the balcony.'

There he goes, bravely sloshing and shouldering through the rain in Gertrude Stein's mac (and it fitted *her* so precisely), too tough to bother with such delicacies as grammar, and developing an ear for conversation, and getting effeminate languages like Italian right, and choosing an expressive vocabulary, and sparing the reader the awkwardness of those three occurrences of the verb *to come* in that sentence and a half about the rain, and discovering subtler and more effective ways of constructing prose than just stringing the bits together with *and*. Hemingway's had a good run: *A Farewell To Arms* was No. 2 in Penguins (No. 1 being André Maurois's *Ariel*) in 1935; in 1966 Penguin were pursuing a pan-Hemingway campaign, deifying him with a white bust à la Beethoven in bookshop windows. Shouldn't we now recognize him as a footnote to the minor art of Gertrude Stein, an appendix to the biography of the great novelist Scott Fitzgerald, and the Ouida of the thirties? Wasn't it enough for Hemingway that, having stolen Gertrude Stein's style and mutilated it, he made a fortune and a name while she was scarcely known except to be scorned? Did he have to attempt also the impossible task of proving he was more manly than she was?